AN ANATOMY OF HUMOR

AN ANATOMY OF HUMOR

Arthur Asa Berger

With a Foreword by
William Fry, Jr.

Transaction Publishers
New Brunswick (U.S.A.) and London (U.K.)

First paperback edition 1998

Copyright © 1993 by Transaction Publishers, New Brunswick, New Jersey.

This book is printed on acid-free paper that meets the American National Standard for Permanence of Paper for Printed Library Materials.

Library of Congress Catalog Number: 92-18197
ISBN: 1-56000-086-4 (cloth); 0-7658-0494-8 (paper)
Printed in the United States of America

Library of Congress Cataloging-in-Publication Data

Berger, Arthur, Asa, 1933–
     An anatomy of humor / Arthur Asa Berger
     Includes bibliographical references and index.
     ISBN 1-56000-086-4 (cloth)
     1. Wit and humor—History and criticism.   2. Wit and humor—Psychological aspects.   I. Title.
PN6147.B47   1992
809.7—dc20   92-18197
                                                                    CIP

For Irving Louis Horowitz and Mary E. Curtis

Contents

Foreword

William F. Fry, Jr.

There have been several strange periods of his life, when Arthur Asa Berger has referred to himself as a Secret Agent. This presentation could be regarded as rather bizarre behavior on the part of a university professor and distinguished man of letters if we are to understand it as intended to be a literal statement of fact. However, even though on the bizarre side, it might be considered plausible, when academia is inspected from a historical perspective and specific cases are counted.

Professor Berger wouldn't be the first scholar to don the invisible uniform and sally forth to collect arcane or privy information for the benefit of some organization or other to which he or she might feel a bond or tie. I am sure that other sociologists or pop culturists or semiologists or behavioral scientists of various persuasions have been the literal type of secret agent on numerous occasions. As a matter of fact, my anthropologist mentor, Gregory Bateson, was a member of the World War II wartime spy organization, OSS, during most of the years of the war in the Pacific. He had done anthropology fieldwork on many of the Southwest Pacific islands in prewar years, was familiar with the territory and had many friends among the island inhabitants. His "Secret Agent" services were of great value to the Allied war efforts against the Axis. Bateson was neither the first nor the last scholarly spy, nor would be Berger.

However, when we turn to gaze upon this professor who thus identifies himself, the potentiality of his performing the role of a literal, authentic Secret Agent fades, and swiftly transmogrifies into something, much more reminiscent of the blathering of an addled mind. Granted that a certain degree of flexibility must be applied when taking appearances into account on this spy business. Wartime spy though he skillfully and beneficially was, Bateson did not present the expected image of Secret Agent. He was tall, over six feet in height, with a craggy handsomeness, emanating prominence and uniqueness; not the appearance usually associated with Secret Agents, who are envisioned as gray, somewhat dumpy, and of medium height, with a doughy flab under their chins and around their belt-lines.

But Berger, although of a quite different sort, looks even more unlikely than Bateson when one weighs the possibilities of his being a functionary mole. Arthur is shorter than medium height; his limbs show a graceful delicateness more frequently associated with a skilled musician or theoretical physicist than with a Secret Agent. Most remarkable, and certainly completely incompatible with the background-blending anonymity necessary for Secret Agent survival, his head is topped with a wildly unruly thatch of bright pink hair. This tint comes from nature, not from a bottle or tube; and it is a standout in any crowd. Further, far from traditional

Secret Agent secretiveness, Arthur is frequently found to be augmenting the impact of nature's gift by indulging his enthusiasm for wearing orange sweatshirts. He also drives an orange automobile. Seeing Arthur driving down the avenue, pink on orange on orange, is a phenomenon impossible to ignore or forget. Surely, few persons aspiring to be true, authentic Secret Agents have worse prospects. Is Berger to be politely, but firmly, escorted into some quiet nook where he can continue to indulge his quaint conceit, sheltered from an unbelieving world, and causing no further shocks to more tender-minded citizens?

Fortunately, this absurdity is resolved in less strenuous fashion by what Professor Berger has written and obscurely published in his sub-basement printshop under the title *The Secret Agent: Essays and Revelations on Media, Popular Culture & Everyday Life in America*. For those who may wish to explore the Professor's mind further on this matter (good luck) and are not privy to a copy of the *Secret Agent* tome, an article entitled "Secret Agent" will be found in the *Journal of Communication* (spring 1974, vol. 24:2) (written by Berger, of course).

Now, what Arthur writes in explaining the meaning of the Secret Agent designation has a great deal of relevance to this present book on humor, as well as having much relevance to many other things. In fact, far from turning out to be an indication of unswerving weirdness on his part, Arthur presents in his Secret Agent concept some remarkably good sense about the roles and performances that are crucial for attaining creativity and significant contribution in scientific careers of any discipline, but most clearly so in the wide range of behavioral sciences—a range that expands almost monthly. The Secret Agent concept is not necessary Arthur's most unique contribution, nor his most outstanding; but it is a very meaty piece, affording nutrition for one's own mental adventuring, and stimulation to set forth in that adventuring. It is a clever and accurate and insightful concept.

In *The Secret Agent*, Berger wrote,

> I really am a secret agent! Not the kind of secret agent who works for governments and steals plans for missiles. I am a self-employed secret agent who searches, relentlessly, for hidden meanings and latent functions. I like to think that, like all secret agents, I shake the very foundations of society. For if society maintains itself on the basis of the unrecognized functions people engage in, when I point out these latent functions I make them recognizable (manifest) and the equilibrium in society is disturbed. . . . Thus I am a secret agent who discovers secrets and broadcasts them . . . to the world. The student of popular culture has the task of analyzing, interpreting, and evaluating whatever it is he is interested. . . . It may be best to think of our culture

as something like an onion, and as we peel away the outer layers, we find ultimately, a core of myth that has shaped everything else.

Although the terminal imagery in the above passage verges a bit into the realm of the chef, rather than that of secret agent, the general meaning of the passage makes quite clear what Berger is all about in calling himself a Secret Agent. Further clarification is offered in his article entitled "Humor and Teaching." "[I suggest] to my students that I see the everyday world. . . as full of secrets, mysteries, etc. which I'm out to discover and make known to others."

These passages make it clear that Berger is not to be taken literally in his statement about being a Secret Agent. This is clearly an artistic use of metaphor—a sort of poetic statement that must be regarded similarly as when we speak or write of the "dancing water" or a "faithless moon." Berger may do things that resemble the behavior of a true Secret Agent, but the context, intent, and results are quite different. In other words, it's not the same thing at all. To underline the difference, his Secret Agent badge carries the notations, "artist" and "writer."

This book on humor, for which I have written this Foreword, is a superb example of Professor Berger carrying out his metaphoric role as Secret Agent, turning this time his Holmesian magnifying glass onto a variety of factors active in the field of humor. It is not my role nor privilege to tabulate this variety. That is reserved for the reader. But it is my prerogative to be able to point out some highlights, and to give general comments that may enhance the reader's experience with Berger and humor.

Now that we know what the professor's all about in his Secret Agent bit, we can look for some of those secrets and latencies of which he has written and which, presumably, he is busy revealing to a generally unself-conscious world—that is, if people will read this book with any reasonable degree of care. I must say, en passant, that I have always been amazed by the low intensity of curiosity that people seem to have about themselves and their fellow humans, about the human race. This has been a general observation of mine, but has been sharpened by my career experiences as a practicing psychiatrist, being confronted repeatedly by the specter of people having to be driven by some great anguish into the most exciting adventure of life—self-discovery—and once in it, so often being internally led into thinking and talking about anything but oneself.

In launching my foreword with those comments about the Secret Agent component of Professor Berger, and then backing those introductory comments with an excellent example of how he follows through in the orientation of the Secret Agent, I have set up a certain hazard, which I must now quickly and carefully destroy. That is the hazard of creating in the mind of the eagerly anticipating reader the impression that this book is, indeed, entirely a collection of casework, a research notebook, a portfolio of files and findings, a secret agent's dossier. That is not the full measure of this book's contents. True to his pink-on-orange-on-orange tradition, there is an abundance of Arthur Asa Berger slathered into several of his chapters. Bergerism, as distinct from Secret Agentism, is particularly prominent in those chapters that are review chapters—that is reviews of various examples of humorous literature and drama.

This sleight of hand is quite subtly accomplished in the chapter entitled "Of Mice and Men." Berger starts out by posing some very solid sociology/pop culture/etc.-type questions, in good Secret Agent style. Then he performs an ultimate ploy in completely turning the stage over to the originator of The Mouse (Mickey, of course), "Let's allow Walt Disney himself to describe his (Mickey's) origin. . . ."

This seemingly guileless sequence is backed up by a few statistics and historic sentences; one hardly even notices the Bergerisms beginning to shoulder the Secret Agentisms aside. But as the chapter progresses, there is more and more pink-on-orange-on-orange until Berger ends up with tossing forth, out of his own head, a stunner that would have left poor old Walt floundering on the floor—if he were so unfortunate to still be around. As the chapter progresses, Berger leaves the Secret Agent more and more out in the cold. He wanders through castration, rags and riches, sublimation and psychohistory, power, the grotesque, brickbats, heroes, and finally brings us to the farthest end of the gastrointestinal tract—the anus. This is how the "artist" and "writer" designations get on Berger's "Secret Agent" badge. Berger keeps his promises, even the subliminal ones.

Another chapter that is quite cute in this same fashion is the one entitled "Twelfth Night." Booked as an investigation of "comedic techniques" with "social considerations," the professor starts out very Secret Agentish, quoting a few renowned, learned authorities. Little flashes of pink-on-orange-on-orange peek out from time to time, such as when he suggests—somewhat hesitantly—that there might be interpretations other than that which one of the authorities has rather pedantically announced in his quotation. But, as he was with Walt Disney, he is generous about the stage with these authorities. And he is also generous with William Shakespeare, for this is Shakespeare's *Twelfth Night* that he is reviewing. A fair amount of script is quoted from the play.

It is his choice of script that gives us flashes of pink-on-orange-on-orange. The reader will remember that a good deal of the humor in *Twelfth Night* is derived from two major sources: mistaken and hidden identities, and the character of the "clown" Malvolio. Naturally, since he is secret agenting the "comedic techniques" of the play, Berger focuses a great deal of his attention on these sources, particularly in his choice of script quotations.

A very interesting thing happens as we are reading these immortal words of the Great Bard. We are understandably beguiled by the exquisiteness; they ring with rich beauty in our brain's ears. We fall into a revery, following the rhythm of that script. We swoop; we dip; we glide.

> Disguise, I see, thou art a wickedness,
> Wherein the pregnant enemy does much.
> ....
> O time, thou must untangle this, not I;
> It is too hard a knot for me to untie!

While Malvolio stands around in his yellow stockings, Berger states, "Thus, Malvolio has puffed himself us horrendously and is ripe for having his balloon pricked. It is his megalomania that makes his victimization so delicious." And finally, "we can, alas relate the characters all too easily to our associates and friends, to politicians and celebrities (and perhaps even to ourselves)."

Well, that's a shock! Out of our revery. Dropped from our Shakespearean cloud. And I finish reading the chapter with the darnedest impression. See if you agree with my reaction. Do you also conclude your reading of the chapter with the impression that, somehow, Berger has succeeded in using Shakespeare's words to hoist a certain authority with his own petard ("petar")? And all without any explicit pamphleteering or bombast. Subtle. I view this as a vivid example of Authur (no *sic*) Asa Berger.

This subtle authoring in "Twelfth Night" is contrastive with an almost brutal shouldering aside of the Secret Agent's gray disguise in favor of the more explicit style that is found in Berger's Huck Finn chapter.

"Twain's achievement is impressive." "Huck is a good American." "This little episode is a commentary on the duplicity of the people and on the bubble of reputation." ". . . absurdity justifies Jim's trip in the wrong direction and describes the nonesuch; both of these matters have an existential dimension." "Jim's rebuttal is brilliant." "Huck has seen enough of society not to want much more of it." "We can even satisfy those critics who see the quest theme as dominant in American litera-ture—and to be sure there is a quest in *Huckleberry Finn*, though it is for something a bit less tangible than the Holy Grail." "The alienation from society, then, is not a symptom of personality loss but of Huck's authen-ticity. . . ." "We learn that we must be skeptical. This does not mean that we must doubt everything, for absolute skepticism is untenable. . . ."

So, in this chapter, and in others in this book, we discover the Secret Agent costume being put aside, and Berger putting himself on the firing line. The Huck Finn chapter has its own unique quality of being thusly explicit, but in such a way as to inspire *con*versation and *con*troversy, rather than subdue or drown them. One is invited to a debate—as participant.

As we feast, in Professor Berger's book, on a range of styles of presentation, so we also are ordering up an even wider menu of humor types and contexts. Many of the published humor studies that I have previously read have had more narrowly focused orientations. Not to express a pejorative on this. It is simply that Berger's book deals with a wide range of humor, and others with more specifically chosen subjects. Remaining in the gustatory metaphor, this book is more like Auntie Mame's smorgasbord, with a dish for any taste, for any occasion.

The richness of content implied by the smorgasbord image is matched on a more microcosmic scale by a feature of the book that I cannot conclude my remarks without mentioning. That feature is Berger's "Glossary of the Techniques of Humor". This glossary is rather like walking along the smorgasbord table and suddenly, unexpectedly coming upon a section of the feast that consists of a fascinating assortment of delicious-looking little dishes that could—if you were to allow yourself to be so beguiled—preoccupy your appetite to at least temporary neglect of the rest of the goodies.

The inclusion of this glossary in this book is very daring, courageous, on Arthur's part. He takes the risk that the volume might become known as the "glossary" book. The nature of this unique contribution is such that an explosion of new avenues of thought about humor can result. It is possible to imagine a myriad of innovative research studies developing from the impetus provided by consideration of implications of the glossary, and especially its various separate categories—each one a potential volume in itself—and some of the more traditional ones have actually been volumes, such as satire and irony. A little potent package.

And perhaps this glossary ties it all together for this particular book of Arthur Asa Berger. The glossary is a potent literary expression of Berger's own views of the various "techniques" of humor. It is his artistic collation of these "techniques." Berger presents an explicit and powerful statement of his knowledge and thoughts in this glossary. It is not tiptoe, hush-hush item. No sneaking around. Here are the artist and the writer in the center of the stage, in full spotlight

But also, remember the mission of Berger's Secret Agent—the shaking of "the very foundations of society." Arthur insists that he is not the sort of secret agent who goes for missiles. But I believe that his glossary will produce some fireworks as time goes on. And so this contribution irreversibly unites the Secret Agent with the artist and the writer.

Acknowledgments

I owe a special debt of gratitude to Irving Louis Horowitz, who has been kind enough (some might say courageous enough and others foolhardy enough) to publish a number of my books. We've had a long and wonderful relationship, though he complains at times that I write too many letters. I also appreciate the kind words of the referee for this book (whose name I do not know) who gave it a positive and perceptive review.

My chapter "Comics and Popular Culture" appeared first in a slightly different form in *The World & I*. This article appeared in the July 1990 issue and is reprinted with permission from *The World & I*, a publication of The Washington Times Corporation, copyright (c) 1990. My chapter on Mickey Mouse and Krazy Kat appeared in *Gay People, Sex and the Media* (1991, copyright (c) Haworth Press, 10 Alice Street, Binghamton, N.Y. 13904), edited by Michelle A. Wolf and Alfred P. Kielwasser. The lines from *The Bald Soprano* are reprinted by permission of Grove/Wiedenfeld. There are a few other previously published essays, all of which have been rewritten for this book. The introductory essay on the social and psychological implications of humor is adapted from an article that originally appeared in an issue of *American Behavioral Scientist*, January/February 1987, Sage Publications on humor that I edited. And my essay on humor and health is a revision of an essay that originally appeared in a book on information and behavior, published by Transaction Publishers. The essay on *Huckleberry Finn* is a revised version of an essay that appeared in the *Mark Twain Journal*. (1976).

Let me also express my appreciation to Bill Fry, the well-known chimp tickler, for his fine foreword. I've benefited greatly from the work of Sigmund Freud, Alan Dundes, Martin Grotjahn, Northrop Frye, Brom Weber, Harry Levin, Tom Inge, Victor Raskin, Rabbi Mordecai Rindenow, Aaron Wildavsky, Mike Noll, Dave Noble, Larry Mintz, Avner Ziv, William Fry, Harvey Mindess, and, of course, all the wonderful comedians, comic strip artists, playwrights, and novelists, who have provided material for me to analyze.

I come from a family of clowns and comedians. My brother Jason, an artist, is a compulsive and, many would say, perfectly obnoxious punster (in French, German, Yiddish and Portugese). My mother told filthy jokes on her deathbed. One of my uncles was an Anglophile poseur. ("I want to look like I might be president of Princeton," he used to say, and he did. In fact he probably looked more like the president of Princeton than the president of Princeton does.) My uncle used two names (Jack Savel, his real name, and Jackson Gregory Savelle, his "English aristocratic" name) and could write backward as well as forward at the same speed. And my father confirmed my suspicions that I was really from royal stock. "Your highness," he would say. "It's time to take out the garbage."

There's a lot of humor in this book and a good deal of analysis of humor in terms of its social and political significance. My glossary is, I believe, an original contribution to the understanding of what makes people laugh and can be used not only to analyze humor but also to create it. I've always felt that creativity and analysis are linked together, and I deal with that subject in an essay in this book. I hope you will enjoy this book and will come away from it not feeling that "Berger hath murdered humor" but with a better understanding and more profound appreciation of humor, in its many forms.

Introduction:
Humor, Psyche, and Society

Humor is everywhere. It insinuates itself into every aspect of our lives and sticks its big nose (Kilroy was here/ Kill-the-Roi, the king/father killer was here) in where we don't want it. It is delicious and yet, at the same time, often painful. We find humor in our conversations, in the movies, on the television screen, in books, in newspapers, in magazines, in comic strips and comic books, on the radio, in the graffiti on our bathroom walls. There is no escaping humor and there is no subject, whether it be sex, marriage, politics, religion, education, work, sports—you name it—that has not been ridiculed, joked about, and used or abused one way or another, as grist for someone's comic militancy.

Our rear ends are the butts of a thousand jokes, as are our other parts, private and not-so-private. Indeed, our most intimate relationships, our most personal problems and our most sacred beliefs provoke humor and have done so for thousands of years.

Two Jewish women are out walking. "Oy" says one to the other. "My son . . . he's a source of pain . . . but also of pleasure." "How is he a source of pain?" inquires the second woman. "He's a homosexual" replies the first woman. "And how is he a source of pleasure?" "He's going with a doctor."

St. Peter is busy minding the gate to heaven when he is called away. He asks Jesus to mind the gate for a while. While Jesus is there an old Italian man appears. "I'm looking for my son," says the man. "I loved him very much and he disappeared. I've been all over the world and asked many people if they had seen him. Everyone said they had heard of him but never had met him . . . " With tears welling in his eyes Jesus opens his arms and exclaims "Father." The old man embraces him and cries "Pinnochio."

We delight, for mysterious reasons, in comic revelations about the inadequacies of the great as well as the absurdity of those all about us. We may even enjoy jokes at our own expense—unless there is too much of a loss of dignity and we feel, too directly, the hostility that is hidden in this humor.

All of us can probably recall incidents in our lives that were funny and which made us feel good. And that seems to be one of the most important

1

aspects of humor—it gives us pleasure, even if it does so often in rather complicated ways. We even seem to derive pleasure figuring out how humor gives us pleasure.

Why We Laugh

Humor is a subject that has attracted the attention and interest of some of our greatest minds, from Aristotle and Kant to Bergson and Freud. It has also fascinated and played an important part in the work of our greatest writers such as Cervantes, Shakespeare, Moliere, Swift and Twain. One could cite many others.

Yet, curiously, after thousands of years spent trying to understand humor, there is still a great deal of controversy about what humor is or why something is funny. There are, however, some important theories on this matter which I would like to discuss here. I will start with *superiority* theories.

For Aristotle, comedy (and I will use the terms humor and comedy interchangeably, though comedy is, technically speaking, a literary form) is based on "an imitation of men worse than the average," of people who are "ridiculous." Hobbes, in a classic formulation, carried the same idea a bit further. As he put it in *The Leviathan*, "The passion of laughter is nothing else but sudden glory arising from a sudden conception of some eminency in ourselves by comparison with the infirmity of others, or with our own formerly."

Hobbes was primarily a political philosopher and author of the classic book *The Leviathan*. It might seem a bit strange for a political philosopher to speculate about humor, but the relationship between humor and power is one that has attracted a considerable amount attention in recent years. That is because we now can see that humor can be a subtle and powerful means of social control by dominant elements in society. And it is, at the same time, a force for resistance by subordinate elements in society. It is only natural, then, that Hobbes, being a philosopher of power, was interested in humor and its utility for those in power. (The relationship between humor and power will be discussed in more detail in various chapters of the book.)

In addition to the matter of superiority, Hobbes also mentions the importance of timing—the sudden glory that is based on a sudden conception. This is an important insight.

A farmer and a professor shared a seat on a train. They found it hard to converse so, to while away the time, the professor suggested they play a game of riddles for a dollar a game. "That's not fair," said the farmer. "I'll play you a dollar against your fifty cents, then," said the professor. "Okay," said the farmer. "You go first," said the professor. The farmer thought for a minute and then said, "what animal has three legs when it walks and two when it flies?" The professor thought for a moment, and then said "I give up." He handed the farmer a dollar. "What's the answer?" asked the professor. "I don't know," said the farmer, handing the professor fifty cents.

A little black girl smears her face with white cold cream. She runs to her mother in the kitchen saying "Mommy, mommy, look at me." Her mother tells her to wipe the cold cream off her face. She then finds her father who tells her the same thing. Upset and pouting she goes to the bathroom, thinking, "I haven't been white for more than a couple of minutes and I already hate two niggers."

There is another theory that is probably the most important and most widely accepted of the explanations of humor. This is the *incongruity* theory of humor which argues that all humor involves some kind of a difference between what one expects and what one gets. The term "incongruity" has many different meanings—inconsistent, not harmonious, lacking propriety and not conforming, so there are a number of possibilities hidden in the term. Incongruity theories involve the intellect, though they may not seem to at first sight— for we have to recognize an incongruity before we can laugh at one (though this recognition process takes place very quickly and is probably done subconsciously).

Incongruity theorists would argue that superiority theories are really special forms of incongruity. Thus, the jokes about the farmer and professor and the little black girl really turn on incongruities, reflected in the punch line, and not superiority, per se.

One of the more interesting and controversial theories of humor stems from the work of Freud. The *psychoanalytic* theory of humor argues that humor is essentially masked aggression (often of a sexual nature) which gives us gratifications we desperately crave. As Freud wrote in his classic book *Jokes and Their Relation to the Unconscious*, "and here at last we can understand what it is that jokes achieve in the service of their purpose. They make possible the satisfaction of an instinct (whether lustful or hostile) in the face of an obstacle that stands in its way" (1963, 101).

In the case of smutty jokes, Freud tells us, we get pleasure because women will not tolerate "undisguised sexuality," so we mask our sexual aggressiveness by humor. We also derive pleasure camouflaging our aggression and hostility (and thus evading the strictures of our super-egos) or regressing to child-like stages, among other things.

Freud's analysis of humor devotes a good deal of attention to the formal or structural properties of jokes. It is not only their subjects that are important but also the forms and the techniques they employ, such as wordplay, condensation and displacement. He also recounts a number of wonderful Jewish jokes in the book and alludes to the remarkable amount of self-criticism found in jokes which Jews tell about themselves. (Jewish humor will be treated in some detail elsewhere in this book.)

"Incidentally," he wrote, "I do not know whether there are many other instances of a people making fun to such a degree of its own character" (1963, 112). His use of the word "fun" is important. He did not regard Jewish jokes as masochistic. Just the opposite.

> Two Jews meet in the neighborhood bath house. "Have you taken a bath? "What?" asked the other. "Is one missing?"

> The bridegroom was most disagreeably surprised when the bride was introduced to him and drew the broker on one side and whispered his remonstrances. "Why have you brought me here?" he asked reproachfully. "She's ugly and old, she squints and has bad teeth and bleary eyes . . . " "You needn't lower your voice," interrupted the broker, "she's deaf as well."

> A Jew noticed the remains of some food in another's beard. "I can tell what you had to eat yesterday." "Well, tell me." "Lentils, then." "Wrong: the day before yesterday."

This "fun" which the Jews make of their character is connected to their social marginality and is, in truth, an effective means of countering and dealing with the difficulties they have faced in trying to live in societies which have frequently been very hostile. It might be argued that since humor is an effective way of keeping in touch with reality, Jewish humor has been intimately connected with Jewish survival. There is, we can see here, an important social dimension to humor. It is not some kind of an idle and trivial matter but generally enables people to gain valuable insights into social and political matters.

There is another theory of humor to consider, and that might be described as the *conceptual* (or even semiotic) theory. It argues that humor is best understood as dealing with communication, paradox, play and the resolution of logical problems. This, at least, is the argument of many cognitive theorists (though Freud also concerned himself with cognitive jokes which suggests that he had cognition covered in his psychoanalytic theory of humor).

William Fry, a psychiatrist who worked with Gregory Bateson at one time, has explained how paradox is related to humor. He writes, in *Sweet Madness*,

> During the unfolding of humor, one is suddenly confronted by an explicit-implicit reversal when the punch line is delivered. The reversal helps distinguish humor from play, dreams, etc. . . . But the reversal also has the unique effect of forcing upon the humor participants an internal redefining of reality. Inescapably the punch line combines communication and meta-communication. (1963, 158)

Thus, at one stroke, the punch line in jokes gives us information which, if the joke is a good one, tells us about the world, strikes us as funny, and functions as a meta-communication (that tells us that what we have heard is "unreal").

The semiotic theory of humor is allied to the cognitive theory. Semiotics asks how meaning is generated in daily life and, for our purposes, in any text. It seeks to answer this question by analyzing the signification found in a given text and by trying to elicit the polar oppositions (or sets of paired opposites) implicit in any work. It also seeks to understand the way the narrative functions (when there is one). These two operations involve investigating the paradigmatic (or oppositional) and the syntagmatic (or linear, narrative) aspects of the text. According to the French anthropologist Claude Lévi-Strauss, the syntagmatic analysis of a text tells us the manifest content, what the text (in this case, joke or other form of humor) is about, and the paradigmatic analysis tells us the latent content, what the joke "really" means. And this meaning is hidden; it is not the same as the subject of the joke or work of humor or text.

To see how these different theories of humor work I will recount a joke and analyze it from the various perspectives described above.

Four Theorists Deconstruct a Joke

I will number each sentence or unit of meaning in the following joke so it will be easy to identify it in the discussion to follow.

The Tan

1. A man goes to Miami for a vacation.
2. After a few days there he looks in a mirror and notices he has a beautiful tan all over his body, with the exception of his penis.

3. He decides to remedy the situation, and have a perfect tan all over his body. So the next morning he gets up early, goes to a deserted section of the beach, undresses, and starts putting sand over his body until only his penis remains exposed to the sun.
4. A couple of little old ladies happen to walk by shortly after the man has finished shoveling the sand all over himself.
5. One notices the penis sticking out of the sand. She points it out to her friend.
6. "When I was twenty, I was scared to death of them."
7. "When I was forty, I couldn't get enough of them."
8. "When I was sixty, I couldn't get one to come near me."
9. "And now they're growing wild on the beach!"

I do not tell jokes well, I must admit, but I find that when I tell this joke during lectures on humor or on other occasions, people generally find it very amusing. Why?

From the point of view of superiority theorists, it would be because we feel superior to various characters in this story. The man who feels he must cover every inch of his body with a tan, at any cost (so to speak) is obviously very foolish and the woman who thinks penises are growing wild on the beach is mistaken, at best, and perhaps even stupid? Segment 9 of the joke, "And now they're growing wild on the beach" is the punch line and can be taken, given our comic context, as a revelation of ignorance. And the segments preceding it reveal a good deal about her sexuality and frustration.

For the incongruity theorist, the fundamental absurdity of a penis sticking out of the sand instead of being between a man's legs, where it belongs (in the first place) and of a person thinking that penises can grow wild on the beach, like wildflowers (in the second place) is the source of the humor. One expects penises to behave and stay shielded from public scrutiny. The punch line, statement 9, generates the incongruity. It postulates penises growing like wild flowers or vegetables, dissociated from male bodies. People's so-called private parts never get tanned as well as the rest of their bodies and it is incongruous to expose these private parts to the public. The joke, then, hinges on the incongruity of seeing private parts in public places.

To the psychoanalytic critic, the humor generated by the joke stems primarily from its sexual content. The humor is related to sexuality and the matter of sexual development in people and, in particular, to sexual hunger. The punch line represents a kind of wish-fulfillment, a sexually paradisiacal state for this woman, where penises grow wild on the beach and are thus easily obtainable and in as great a quantity as may be desired.

Sexual repression, which Freud postulated as being the price we pay for civilization, is no longer a dominating force.

The man, it could be argued, also has unconscious exhibitionist tendencies which are masked by his alleged desire (fixation?) to obtain an even tan on every part of his body. There may also be a regressive aspect to the woman, who does not seem to know that penises always come attached to men—a means, a good Freudian might argue, of escaping from penis envy. Although this joke may be connected to psychological processes in individuals, it also has a very strong social component, and refers to the problems of sexuality amongst the aged, among other things.

From the cognitive perspective, the joke establishes a play frame which is generated by the man's bizarre behavior—his desire to tan every inch of his body. This play frame allows us to view the crazy notion that penises might grow wild on the beach as humorous, something not to be taken seriously. The semiotic analysis of this joke shows something else.

Line number 9, the punch line, "and now they're growing wild on the beach" sets up a paradigmatic opposition which contrasts nature with culture. We can see this in the chart that follows:

Nature/Culture Polarity in the Tan Joke

Nature	Culture
Growing Wild	Sexuality at 20,40,60
the beach	society
free sexuality	repression

It is this set of polar oppositions that gives us an insight into the real meaning of the joke. Whether people recognize this at the conscious level is beside the point.

It is obvious that there are similarities between the psychoanalytic perspective, which argues that jokes (and works of humor in general) deal with unconscious phenomena (such as drives) and the semiotic perspective, which suggests that people may not consciously understand the real meaning of narratives, in general, and jokes in particular. In much contemporary thought about literature and the arts there are numerous alliances between psychoanalytic and semiotic critics, so this similarity should not surprise us.

A Fifth Interpretation of the Tan Joke

[5]   There is a political dimension to the tan joke that is worth considering. If we examine the joke, we find a number of attitudes or values reflected in it, all of which have political implications. For example, we find ridicule directed toward the man, who lies on the beach, naked, and pours sand on himself until only his penis is showing. And we find ridicule directed towards the woman (and by implication, the aged in general) who still has sexual desires but is frustrated. We often find humor connected with frustrating sexual impulses and activities in people, and should not overlook the matter of power, here. The old frequently try (generally with little success) to control the sexuality of the young and dominate their sexual lives as well as other aspects of their lives.

There is also a political dimension to the ridiculing of the utopianism of the old woman. A society without repression, where penises grow wild on the beach and sexuality is free and uninhibited by social constraints, is, the joke suggests, absurd. There is, then, a conservative impulse in this joke. Contemporary feminist discourse often uses the term "phallocentric" to deal with society, the media and the arts and the way they are dominated by men and male values. Could one find a more phallocentric text than the tan joke. In this joke, the women are frustrated sexually and not terribly intelligent, either. From a feminist perspective, it is an excellent example of the way males dominate females.

We have to consider, when we look at humor from a political perspective, who is doing the laughing and who is being laughed at. We would do well to consider the status of the laugher (high or low) and the direction of the laughter (we laugh at others, others laugh at us).

The following chart deals with these relationships.

Status and Direction of Laughter
Direction of Laughter

		We Laugh at Others	Others Laugh at Us
Power & Status of Laugher	High	Equality	Persuasion
	Low	Resistance	Control

This diagram yields four groups of people:

- those with high status who direct laughter towards others, yielding a sense of equality;

- those with low status who laugh at others and in so doing resist control or domination via humor;

- those with high status who laugh at us or direct laughter at us (an attempt at persuasion);

- those with low status who are laughed at by others and are subject to control and domination by this laughter.

The ability to direct laughter at individuals, groups, institutions, ideas, what you will, is really a form of power, even though we may not generally recognize the coercive nature of this laughter. It is insidious because generally speaking we do not recognize what is happening. When a politician becomes the object of general ridicule (as in the case of Quayle and all the Quayle jokes), he has serious problems.

The Comic and the Tragic

One reason humor, in its various forms, formats, and manifestations, has intrigued our best minds—and plays so important a role in the work of our greatest writers—is that humor is terribly important to people. There is a widespread misconception among the general public that humor is, somehow, trivial and not worth serious concern. For some reason, perhaps connected to our Puritan heritage, we've been led to think that tragedy is serious stuff and that comedy (and humor in general) is mere entertainment, a diversion from the truly important and "solemn" things in life.

Fortunately this kind of thinking is being challenged. We might make an analogy with dreams here. Once, not too long ago, dreams were seen as insignificant—interesting phenomena but not worth much attention. Then Freud came along and suggested that dreams are the royal road to the unconscious. Recent experiments have suggested that dream work is crucial to everyone's good health and mental well-being.

How ironic, then, that this seemingly trivial, inconsequential, common thing we know as humor is so enigmatic and plays so vital a role in our psychic lives and in society.

In order to understand best what humor is, it is useful to contrast it with that which it isn't, with it's opposite. This is best done by taking the literary manifestation of humor, the comic, and comparing it with its opposite, the tragic. For it is in the comic that humor is best known and most easily fathomed, and the comic-tragic relationship is the easiest to understand. In the chart that follows I list the various attributes of the comic and contrast them with the tragic. As a result of this exercise I hope you will understand better what each one is and how they relate to one another.

The Comic	The Tragic
Chance	Inevitability
Freedom	Determinism
Optimism	Pessimism
Survival	Destruction
The Social	The Personal
Integration	Separation
Low Status	High Status
Trivial	Serious
Lowly Characters	Elevated Characters
Pleasure	Pain
Cathexis	Catharsis

The world of the comic is one of chance, accident, mistakes, and contingency, but these phenomena are not fatal or destructive as they are in the tragic. The comic involves freedom (to make an ass of oneself or someone else) and is essentially optimistic. Comic figures survive while tragic ones are usually carried off the stage, dead.

It has been suggested by many commentators that the comic involves the world of the social and the political and that comedy involves, amongst other things, chastising those who do not know or observe the social codes. Comedy thus has an implicit socializing effect. Tragedy, on the other hand, involves the fall of great individuals, often as a result of hubris or some "tragic flaw" in their character and is more personal than social—though we all learn from the fall of a great man or woman about the nature of life and related matters.

Comedy tends to be about ordinary people or low life, as opposed to the tragic, which involves the great and remarkable (though there is a good deal of debate on this matter) whose "fall" becomes, then, all the more meaningful. The destruction of a king or ruler is tragic; the destruction of a nobody is, generally speaking, seen as more pathetic than tragic. And the comic types—the buffoons, the zanies, the clowns, the fools—they live on and their triumphs over adversity and their revelations about the nature of human stupidity and absurdity provide great pleasure. The tragic hero, I suggest, provides catharsis; the comic hero provides cathexis. With the tragic hero we have a powerful emotional experience, a purgation, caused by our ability to empathize with the tragic hero and our recognition of the fate that ultimately awaits each of us.

The comic hero, on the other hand, provides us with a cathexis, a release of pent-up energy, which often has a libidinal aspect to it and which is generally life-affirming and celebratory. For we learn, from comedy, how strange people are, how consumed they are often are with petty jealousies, with delusions, fantasies, etc. And yet these flaws which we find in others (and can assume may be found in ourselves) are not destructive. Instead, they are instructive. The laughter that comedy evokes in us is, in large measure, connected to the relief of a tension that has been built up about how some "mess" that the comic figures have got themselves into will be resolved. Our laughter suggests a recognition that somehow we will all survive—even if somewhat battered and deflated. In the ecology of the psyche, humor is instrumental and of enormous importance.

A Spoof

Let me conclude with some items from a parody of course descriptions that might be found in a catalogue from some institution offering courses dealing with the "human potential." What follows is a selection of course titles taken from a mimeographed sheet entitled "Professional Growth Courses" that a student handed me after one of my lectures. This little satire on the human potential movement shows that a healthy skepticism and sense of humor still exists in many of our students. The course titles speak for themselves.

C100   Creative Suffering

C101   Overcoming Peace of Mind

C103   Guilt Without Sex

C104   The Primal Shrug

C105   Ego Gratification Through Violence

C106   Molding Your Child's Behavior Through Guilt and Fear

C300   I Made $100 in Real Estate

C350   Creative Tooth Decay

C366   High Fiber Sex

C380   Looters Guide to American Cities

C400   How to Draw Genitalia

C450   The Repair and Maintenance of Your Virginity

C500   Christianity and the Art of RV Maintenance

PART ONE

THEORETICAL CONCERNS

1

A Glossary of the Techniques of Humor: Morphology of the Joke-Tale

What sits in a tree and jumps on girls?
Jack the Grape.
What sits in a tree and jumps on boys?
Jack the Grapefruit.

What follows is a catalogue, in alphabetical order, of the basic techniques of humor. What I will do is list as many of these techniques as I have been able to discover (in an examination and analysis of a number of different works of humor), provide examples of the technique, and explain how the technique functions. This will give us a means of taking any example of humor (created at any time, in any genre, in any medium) and showing *what* it is that generates the humor and provokes (often) laughter—or whatever state it is that we feel when we encounter something humorous.

Since works of humor are often incredibly complex, we will frequently find a number of different mechanisms operating at the same time, though one mechanism is often dominant. At times some of my explanations of a given technique will be fairly extended, but I have tried to be as succinct as I can possibly be in most cases.

I have used jokes (for the most part) in this glossary for two reasons. First, they are short and easy to reproduce, and second, they enable me to deal with the techniques of humor in an immediate and direct manner. But let me emphasize that I do NOT believe that telling jokes is a good way for the average person to be funny. A joke, as I understand it and as it has been traditionally defined, *is a story with a punch line—that is used for comic effect*. When you tell a joke you are, in essence, generally performing someone else's material. Some people can do this very well, but many can't. (That is why I was tempted to give this glossary a subtitle—"How To Be Funny Without Telling Jokes for Those Who Tell Jokes Without Being Funny.") I believe it is through the use of the various techniques listed and explained in this glossary that people can create their own humor. So why use other people's?

In certain respects this glossary is similar to Vladimir Propp's pathbreaking book, *Morphology of The Folktale*. In this book Propp listed a number of what he called "functions" (actions of characters as they relate to the plot) and these "functions" are, he argued, at the heart of all narratives. They are the building blocks on which stories are constructed. I had not read Propp when I prepared my glossary, but I realized, like him, that the subject matter of a story or joke was frequently irrelevant. It was often the case that a given joke I found had different subjects. A joke in one joke book was about a minister and the same joke, in a different book, was about a professor.

If subject or theme wasn't all important, then, I concluded, technique was and so I elicited as many techniques of humor as I could find, not asking *why* something was funny (we may never really know) but *what* was it that generated the humor. I might point out that we must always consider reversals of techniques, though I do not deal with this in the glossary. Thus, if exaggeration is one important technique, so is the negative or reverse form of this, understatement. Both involve exaggeration, but in different directions, so to speak.

In the "Jack the Grapefruit" joke there are a number of humorous techniques at work. It has an element of facetiousness about it, with a character with a bizarre name, Jack the Grape. We find the word "rape" buried in this name, so there are allusions involving sexuality. In the second part of this joke there is an allusion to Jack's homosexuality, in which Grape is tied to "fruit," a slang term for homosexual males. A grapefruit is not a Grapefruit. With the capital "G" a grapefruit becomes a homosexual. The form of this "joke" is a riddle—but I am not concerned, in my Glossary, with forms since I believe techniques are more basic than forms. A riddle can be turned into a standard joke ("Did you hear about this character who sits on trees and jumps on girls? His name is Jack the Grape.") What is more important is the nonsense, the word-play, and other techniques.

The analysis of humor (and of jokes in particular) should involve the following steps:

1. breaking down the example of humor used into its main elements or components—that is, isolating the various techniques used to generate the humor;

2. Rating the techniques—deciding which technique is basic and which techniques are secondary.

This is based on the assumption that humor has a process aspect to it which can be separated into various parts and analyzed. Any example of humor "shields" various techniques that generate the humor, and something is funny or humorous, in the final analysis, not because of the subject matter or theme but because of the techniques employed by whomever created the humor. There are four basic categories under which all my techniques of humor can be subsumed:

1. *Language*. The humor is verbal.

2. *Logic*. The humor is ideational.

3. *Identity*. The humor is existential.

4. *Action*. The humor is physical or nonverbal.

These categories are useful in that they give us a sense of what kind of humor is being produced, but the techniques are the essential matter to consider in analyzing humor. (Almost all of the techniques described in this glossary are functional, but some, such as Burlesque, are really classificatory and are included so as to provide the reader with a sense of how certain techniques of humor relate to one another. In the Burlesque section, for example, it is the techniques listed under this catch-all technique, that are functional.)

While I'm not perfectly satisfied with the list of techniques that is to follow (and the jokes and other humor used to exemplify each technique), the glossary does offer us an opportunity to understand the mechanisms at work in humor—and, by implication, to use these techniques to generate our own humor, should we desire to do so. That is why I have given this chapter the subtitle "Morphology of the Joke-Tale." It is an allusion to Propp but it is also a good description of what I have done.

Language	Logic	Identity	Action
Allusion	Absurdity	Before/After	Chase
Bombast	Accident	Burlesque	Slapstick
Definition	Analogy	Caricature	Speed
Exaggeration	Catalogue	Eccentricity	Time
Facetiousness	Coincidence	Embarrassment	
Insults	Disappointment	Exposure	
Infantilism	Ignorance	Grotesque	
Irony	Mistakes	Imitation	
Misunderstanding	Repetition	Impersonation	
Over literalness	Reversal	Mimicry	
Puns, Word Play	Rigidity	Parody	
Repartee	Theme/Variation	Scale	
Ridicule		Stereotype	
Sarcasm		Unmasking	
Satire			

Categories and Techniques of Humor

These techniques were elicited by making a content analysis of all kinds of humor in various media and are, as classification schemes should be, comprehensive and mutually exclusive. I've not been able to find other techniques of humor to add to my list. The focus on techniques means that I treat certain topics, such as parody, as a technique rather than a form or a genre. I have done so because I think that recognizing techniques is more important than using traditional categories.

Absurdity, Confusion, and Nonsense (logic)

Didn't I meet you in Buffalo?
No, I never was in Buffalo.
Neither was I. Must have been two other fellows.

Why do elephants paint their toenails red?
So they can hide in cherry trees.

Have you even seen an elephant in a cherry tree?
No.
It must work, then.

What is it that hangs on the wall in bathrooms and one can dry one's hands on?
A towel.
No! A herring.
But for goodness sakes, a herring doesn't hang on a wall.
You can hang one there if you want to.
But who would dry his hands on a herring?
You don't have to . . .

Absurdity and its related forms—confusion and nonsense—seems to be relatively simple, but it is not . . . and its effects may be quite complicated, as Freud pointed out in his discussion of nonsense humor. Absurdity works by making light of the "demands" of logic and rationality as we traditionally know them. This absurdity doesn't necessarily take the form of silliness (though in many children's jokes it does) but may be an example of a relatively sophisticated philosophical position.

If life is absurd, as many existentialists suggest, then the humor of absurdity can be seen as a means towards realism: an understanding of humanity's predicament and our possibilities in an irrational universe. This explains why the plays of Beckett and Ionesco (and others) fascinate us and speak to us in such a profound manner.

In the Buffalo joke, our sense of order and intelligibility are played with. There are two tricks played upon us. First, the man who claimed to have met a person in Buffalo reveals that he had never been there. But if that was all there was to the joke it would be relatively flat. The last phrase, "it must have been two other fellows," pushes the joke into the absurd.

The second joke plays with logic and reasoning processes. It is asserted that elephants paint their toenails red so they can hide in cherry trees. When it is confirmed that elephants have never been seen hiding in cherry trees, this is taken as proof of the assertion. Our attention is redirected from the ridiculous nature of the proposition to its seeming truthfulness.

The third joke deals with our sense of possibility and probability. It is unlikely that one would dry one's hands in a bathroom (or anywhere) with a herring hanging on the wall, but is possible or conceivable that one might wish to do so. The last line, "you don't have to," turns the humor back on the reasonable person; he becomes foolish by virtue of his good sense on normality.

We all seem to need to impose our sense of logic and order on the world, and when we come across situations or instances where our logic doesn't work, we react by being puzzled and, in certain cases, amused.

Accident (logic)

"Ladies and Gentlemen, The President of the United States . . . Hoobert Heever."

Newspaper Headlines:
Thugs Eat/ Then Rob Proprieter
Officer Convicted Of Accepting Bride

Advertisement:
Sheer stockings—designed for dressy wear, but so serviceable that many women wear nothing else.

In my classification system I have distinguished among three seemingly similar yet different ways or producing humor: Accidents, Mistakes (or Errors), and Coincidences. The first of these methods is demonstrated by the material reproduced above. It stems from things like slips of the tongue (fluffs), letters left off or improperly placed in headlines (typos), inadvertent and ambiguous constructions of sentences, etc.

An accident is different from a mistake or an error. A mistake stems from ignorance or imprudence while an accident is essentially a matter of chance. A coincidence involves a chance correspondence of some kind, that generally leads to some embarrassment, but need not involve error. We find accidents humorous as long as they are not serious and do not generate strong anxiety.

Allusions (language)

A Lieutenant was given two weeks leave to go on his honeymoon. At the end of his leave he wired his commanding officer: "It's wonderful here. Request another week's extension of leave." He received the following reply. "It's wonderful anywhere. Return immediately."

A troupe of actors come into a county to perform a number of plays by Shakespeare. The Sheriff of the county tells them that they cannot advertise the plays they will be presenting. The director of the troupe puts a sign up at the theatre and everyone knows what plays will be shown.

l. Wet   *2. Dry*
    3. Miscarriage
4. 3"   *5. 6"*   *6. 9"*

What were the plays?
l. Midsummer's Night's Dream
2. Twelfth Night
3. Love's Labor Lost
4. Much Ado About Nothing
5. As You Like It
6. The Taming of the Shrew

Allusions are the bread and butter of everyday humor and are very much tied to social and political matters as well as situations which have a sexual dimension (and sometimes, of course, to both). It is, in fact, the allusiveness of much of our humor that makes it such a useful and important means of getting at a given society's interests and preoccupations. In some cases, such as well publicized scandals, etc. just the mention of a person's name is enough to evoke laughter. There is an element, here, of an unsuccessful attempt, on the part of the person involved in the scandal, to escape from embarrassment.

The joke about the Lieutenant is based on the conventional joy of sexual relations. The humor in the joke revolves around a misunderstood allusion. We must assume that the honeymooning officer meant by "it" the pleasure of life in general when he said "it." But this "it" was interpreted (with good reason, one might add) by the commander to mean "sexual intercourse." Since one of the comic joys of civilized life seems to involve interfering with people's sexual lives and denying them their pleasures, there seems to be an element of spite in the joke.

Allusions are tied to mistakes, errors, gaffes, stupid things people say and do that become known, for one reason or another. They are tied to information that people have. The allusion is a cue which enables us to recall, once again, these mistakes, etc. The event that is alluded to must not be terribly serious or important. If it were, the allusion would not generate humor but, instead, something like pain or anxiety. Thus, our allusions often deal with sexual matters, personality traits, behavioral characteristics, and other matters which may be embarrassing but not painful. We are recalling material that was seen as humorous once and enjoying it once again or we are interpreting things in ways that will generate humor by embarrassing others.

The joke about the Shakespearean plays is a kind of riddle that involves tying the names of plays to various sexual phenomena: wet dreams, being unable to perform sexually, the size of penises, etc. The humor is based on allusions of a sexually disguised nature and stems from seeing connections between a signifier and a play that can be connected to that signifier. Part of the humor also stems from the ability to connect all of the plays to sexuality.

Allusions are consensual forms of humor, then. The allusion tells us what we can legitimately poke fun at and also tells us what people, in general, know about the rich, the famous, the powerful, etc. In the final analysis, allusions suggest that we are all pretty much the same. "To err is human." And to allude to other people's errors is also human.

Analogies, Metaphors, etc. (logic)

> Jack eating rotten cheese did say,
> Like Samson I my thousands slay;
> I vow, quoth Roger, so you do.
> And with the self-same weapon, too.

> (Benjamin Franklin, "Quatrain")

The mechanism at work in the humor of analogy is based on some kind of an invidious comparison. The Franklin poem makes an analogy between Jack and Samson and contains an allusion to Samson's weapon (the jawbone of an ass) which turns out, also, to be an insult. This is generally the case with humorous analogies, for analogies by themselves have no humorous content to them. Either an insult or some other humorous technique is employed along with the metaphor.

In its more sophisticated manifestation, the humor of analogy is used in what is called a "metaphysical conceit." This is an elaborate metaphor in which seemingly incongruous elements are united. It was used with great success by the metaphysical poets such as John Donne and Richard Crashaw. In Donne's "A Valediction Forbidding Mourning," there is a famous conceit comparing lovers to the two legs of a compass:

> If they be two, they are two so
> As stiff twin compasses are two;
> The soul, the fixed foot, makes no show
> To move, but doth if the other do. . . .

There is a humorous aspect to the comparison here, but it is a very subtle, genial kind of humor.

The novel, *Miss Lonelyhearts*, by Nathanael West, has many conceits in it and is based on a conceit—it is about a lonelyhearts columnist with an overwhelming Christ complex. The linking of a male reporter functioning as Miss Lonelyhearts with Christ and of newspapermen with priests is made explicit when one of the characters, Shrike, says "The Miss Lonelyhearts are the priests of twentieth century America."

Before and After: Transformation, Development and Learning (identity)

Before marriage, a man's a dude. After marriage, he's subdued

A man is hitchhiking on a highway when a car pulls over. "Are you a Republican?" asks the driver. "No," says the man. "I'm a Democrat." "Sorry," says the driver of the car, who then pulls off. A short while later another car, driven by a young man in a three-piece suit pulls over. "Are you a Republican?" the driver asks. "No," says the hitchhiker. "Sorry," says the driver, who then drives away. A few minutes after that, a car, driven by a gorgeous blonde, pulls over. "Are you a Republican?" asks the blonde. "Hmm," thinks the hitchhiker, "I'd better say I am since I missed two rides because I said I was a Democrat." "Yes, I'm a Republican," he tells the woman. "Get in," she says, smiling. As they drive off, the hitchhiker looks at the woman and notices how beautiful she is. "Hmm," he thinks. "I've only been a Republican two minutes and I already want to screw someone!"

Before perestroika we were all dogs, wearing muzzles, chained to a two-meter leash, with the food just out of reach. After perestroika the chain was longer, the food dish further away, but we can bark as much as we want.

The "before and after" technique is a commonly used one, often found in plays and movies, to show how characters can transform themselves (or be transformed as in *My Fair Lady*). The change in the person becomes contrasted with the sameness or rigidity of those about them (or mechanicalness, to use a Bergsonian term of reference) and this comparison can be used to generate a great deal of humor. Sometimes the change itself is the source of humor. In *Twelfth Night*, for example, Malvolio changes his behavior (as the result of a letter he has received, which he mistakenly thinks has come from the woman he serves, Olivia) and makes an ass of himself. So before and after change can generate humor two ways—by ridiculing others who do not change and may be very rigid or by ridiculing the person who changes.

The "before marriage" maxim is based on stereotyped conceptions people have about marriage and the "loss of male freedom" and also involves a play on sound: dude/subdued. The hitchhiker joke is more complicated. It is based on the notion that Republicans are rich people who have access to the powerful and take unfair advantage of (that is "screw" politically) the working classes, who tend to be Democrats. But "screw" is an ambiguous term, which also means "have sexual relations with," and in this joke it takes on both meanings.

This joke is very similar in structure to the one reprinted earlier about the little black girl who smears her face with cold cream, thus becoming "white." When her parents get upset at the mess she's made and order her to take the cold cream off she discovers that she's only been white two minutes and already "hates two niggers." In both cases, there are transformations to different identities (political and racial) and attendant changes in beliefs and attitudes. These changes deal with the less powerful and the more powerful and tell us something about political and racial power relationships in our society.

The joke about perestroika alludes to the situation in what used to be called The Soviet Union. The main thing about perestroika, the joke suggests, somewhat cynically, is that people are still, for all intents and purposes, treated like dogs—but now they are allowed to bark. The linkage of dogs not barking and communist control of societies is found in a similar joke.

> A dog swims from Cuba to Miami. When he drags himself on the beach, a number of American dogs gather around him. The American dogs ask him questions. "Did you not get enough food?" they ask. "No," he said, "There was plenty of food." "Did you not get medical attention when you needed it?" they continue. "No," he replies, "There were many excellent veterinarians to take care of me when I was ill." "Well, then," they ask, "Why did you leave?" "Because," he replies, "every once in a while I like to bark."

Not being able to bark is a metaphor, then, for not being free and able to speak one's mind.

Bombast and Rhetorical Exuberance (language)

> A man who owned a garage cut his hand. Several days later it became infected, so he went to the doctor. The doctor explained what had happened in highfalutin medical

technology, treated the cut, and charged ten dollars. The next week, the garage owner's assistant told him that the doctor's car was outside and had a flat tire. The garage owner said "Diagnose it as an absence of flatulence of the perimeter caused by the penetration of a foreign object resulting in the dissipation of the compressed atmospheric contents and charge him accordingly."

> I burn, I more than burn; I am all fire,
> See how my mouth and nostrils flame, expire!
> I'll not come near myself—
> Now I'm a burning lake, it rools and flows;
> I'll rush and pour it all upon my foes.

John Dryden, "Aureng Zebe"

Rhetorical exuberance is a technique of humor that derives its power from its extravagance, from our sense of the difference between what is said and how it is said. There is, in the garage joke, a note of pretentiousness on the part of the doctor who eventually gets some of his own medicine. We have humor of reversal here, along with the inflated language. The exaggeration in the Dryden poem is the source of the humor.

Bombast may be a development of an infantile form of humor, gibberish. In bombast, however, the nonsense has been turned into something meaningful, but the mode of expression, the exaggeration, reveals a joking sensibility. There also may be an element of the infant's joy at his/her mastery of language.

Burlesque (identity)

Burlesque, as a literary form, is a general category like humor. According to M.H. Abrams:

"Burlesque," "parody," "caricature," and "travesty" are often used interchangeably, but to equate the terms in this way is to surrender very useful critical distinctions. It is better to use *burlesque* as the generic term for all literary forms in which people, actions, or other literary works are made ridiculous by incongruous imitation, and to reserve the other terms as names for various species of burlesque. When the laugh is raised (as it often is), not for its own sake, but to deride some person or object existing outside the burlesque itself, burlesque in its various species serves as a vehicle of satire. (1961,9)

Abrams goes on to discuss specific forms of the burlesque in more detail.

Satire, he points out, derides a person or an object, or diminishes a subject "by making it ridiculous and evoking towards it attitudes of amusement, contempt or scorn" (1961, 85). Parody derides a specific literary work or style by imitating its particular features and applying them to trivial matters. "Travesty," he writes, "mocks a specific work by treating lofty subjects in grotesquely extravagant or lowly terms" (1961, 10). By caricature, he means "a type of portrait which makes a person ludicrous by exaggerating or distorting prominent features without losing the likeness" (1961,10) and a lampoon, he suggests, is a "full-length verbal portrait of an individual in which he is ridiculed in a biting and often scurrilous manner" (1961,10).

A number of these topics will be discussed in greater length elsewhere in this glossary. For our purposes, it is best to reserve the term burlesque for a kind of theatrical production featuring sexually provocative skits, slapstick humor and nude or seminude dancers and chorus lines. This is the way it has been traditionally understood.

Caricature (identity)

Caricature is one of the most fundamental techniques of humor, and though it is easily appreciated, since it is based on the principle of comparison and contrast, philosophically speaking, it is not simple. An English author, C.R. Ashbee, quotes Sir Thomas Browne who wrote (in 1690),

> When men's faces are drawn with resemblance to some other animals, the Italians call it to be drawn in Caricaturia.

This idea has been expanded and has led to the basic method of contemporary caricature—the ludicrous and grotesque representation of people by exaggeration of their characteristic features and, at the same time, a retention of likeness. We generally understand caricature to be pictorial, but it need not be so. One can caricature someone verbally, also—by capturing and grotesquely imitating his or her particular style of speaking or writing. (Where caricature ends and parody begins is a difficult question, for both involve imitation; perhaps we can reserve caricature for imitations that have an element of the grotesque about them, that are very strong and biting?)

The psychologist Ernst Kris has suggested, in *Psychoanalytic Explorations in Art*, that drawing caricatures is related to children's joy in drawing and in playing with words and making puns. He sees the famous caricature of Louis Phillipe as a pear as, in essence, a visual pun and believes that this mechanism informs many caricatures.

Catalogues (logic)

> From East Egg, then, came the Chester Beckers and the Leeches, a man named Bunsen, who I knew at Yale, and Doctor Webster Civet, who was drowned last summer up at Maine. And the Nornbeams and the Willie Voltaires, and a whole clan named Blackbuck, who always gathered in a corner and flipped up their noses like goats at whosoever came near. And the Ismays and the Chrystie's (or rather Hubert Auerbach and Mr. Christie's wife), and Edgar Beaver, whose hair, they say, turned cottonwhite one winter afternoon for no good reason at all.

> Clarence Endive was from East Egg, as I remember. He came only once, in white knickerbockers, and had a fight with a bum named Etty in the garden. From farther out on the Island came the Cheadles and the O.R.P. Schraders, and the Stonewall Jackson Abrams of Georgia, and the Fishguards and the Ripley Snells.

> (F. Scott Fitzgerald, *The Great Gatsby*)

The comic catalogue is a standard humorous technique. It is, in essence, a vehicle that makes it possible to use nonsense, funny names and various kinds of incongruities and "hide" all this in the catalogue. In the passage quoted above, Fitzgerald created odd names, inserted material that was quite silly, and satirized what we would call the "beautiful people." He "turned" many people into beasts and plants. Notice that there are leeches, civets (a kind of cat), hornbeams (we must turn the *n* into an *h*), goats, bucks, beavers and fishes. There are also endives, a vegetable. Some of the names are odd, also—the Stonewall Jackson Abrams, the Ripley Snells, O.R.P. Schraeders, and so on.

There is a sense of incongruity at having these "animals" (or representative of lower orders) at a "high class" party. The comic catalogue offers the humorist a golden opportunity to be incongruous, to play with words and sounds by traducing the functionality and logic of the list.

Chase Scenes (action, nonverbal)

There are a number of elements at work in the chase scene. On the most elementary level there is the matter of sheer movement and the possibilities it provides for slapstick, confusion, accidents and comic gesture. The chase usually involves a person who is attempting to avoid being punished or humiliated in some manner. This person must use ingenuity and speed to avoid being caught and much of the humor in chase scenes comes from our pleasure in seeing the person being chased use his or her ingenuity. There also seems to be an element of joy in the physical act of seeing people run away from others, as long as we see this in a comic frame. The chase scene is also a staple of drama, but the comic frame is missing and "life and death" are generally at stake in these chases.

We seem to find it amusing seeing people humorously frustrated (especially when sex is involved); usually this takes the form of a wild variety of bizarre accidents, mistakes, coincidences, etc. that deter would-be lovers from making love. But we also enjoy seeing comic actors "frustrate" those who pursue them.

On the psychological level, the chase involves an "escape" by the id (and an id figure) from the strictures of the superego (and a superego or distorted superego figure). One of the most common elements of the comic chase scene involves the participation of people who are not directly involved in the action. They see someone being chased and join in, increasing the odds against the person being chased and making the narrow escapes and ingenious ploys of the chasee all the more enjoyable.

There are all kinds of possibilities as far as chase scenes are concerned. Buster Keaton is continually chased by all the policemen in town in *Cops*; in other films he is chased by huge boulders, by armies, etc. Chaplin is often chased by huge, brutish men who, we know, want to beat him up. Chase scenes involve action, and are nonverbal. Much humor involves language but there is also humor tied to action, to facial expression and use of the body that we must keep in mind.

Coincidences (logic)

> *A young man was called up for a medical exam by his draft board. When he was examined by the doctor, the young man pretended he couldn't see anything. "Please read that chart," said the doctor. "What chart?" said the young man. "The one on the wall," replied the doctor. "What wall?" asked the young man. The doctor then classified him as 4-F and the young man left. That evening, he decided to celebrate and went to the movies. When the film ended, to his amazement the young man found himself sitting next to the doctor who had examined him. Thinking quickly, the young man asked the doctor, "Is this the line for the bus to Hoboken?"*

The humor of coincidence involves our sense of order in the universe and the way the "fates" work. Coincidence humor is primarily based on embarrassment: circumstances work, by chance, to put one in an awkward situation. The humor either can end there, or can lead to an attempt to escape from embarrassment. I distinguish between coincidence humor and escape from embarrassment humor because one can be put into an embarrassing situation as the result of a mistake or a misunderstanding, and not by chance. Also, a coincidence itself may strike us as funny or "uncanny" or even humorously strange, and not involve embarrassment.

The draft joke involves embarrassment and an attempt to escape from it. From a psychoanalytic perspective, we find an id attempting to avoid the strictures of the superego. Underlying this is a notion that the universe is just and that wrongdoers usually get caught.

Comparisons (logic)

A number of years ago I published a book called The TV-Guided American. *It had chapters on a number of important television programs in the 1970s. In the review of the book that appeared in* The New York Times, *Jeff Greenfield completed his review of my book by suggesting, "Berger is to the study of television what Idi Amin is to tourism in Uganda."*

What's the difference between capitalism and communism? In capitalism, man exploits man. In communism, it's just the opposite.

"Comparisons," as the saying goes, "are odious." That is because most comparisons involve some kind of criticism—either explicit or implicit. Some comparisons are not humorous; it is only when the nature of the comparison is ridiculous or there is another technique at work that comparisons are funny. In the anecdote cited above, it is the insult that generates the humor; Idi Amin murdered countless people and was seen by most everyone as a monster. Thus, Greenfield was saying that I am as bad a writer as Amin is a spokesman who would encourage people to visit Uganda. My telling of the story is an example of "victim" humor, and is also humor of analogy.

Sometimes the aggression and hostility is much more direct and vulgar. In answering the riddle "Name two things that look alike," people who want to be nasty reply "your face and my ass." The comparison of capitalism and communism is a means of ridiculing the egalitarianism that is supposed to exist in communist societies. When one says "man exploits man" in capitalism and it is just the opposite in communism, we are still left with "man exploits man."

Definitions (language)

> A bore: someone who talks when you want him to listen.
>
> (Ambrose Bierce, *Devil's Dictionary*)

> A tree is an object that will stand in one place for years,
> then jump in front of a lady driver.
>
> (Ruth Lemezis)

The humorous definition is a technique which has been used to great advantage through the ages. Ambrose Bierce's *Devil's Dictionary* is one of the more notable collections of humorous definitions and there are many other "left-handed" types of dictionaries, full of comic definitions, that are available.

I see defining something as a technique—one which facilitates the use of other humorous techniques, such as insult or exaggeration. There is an element of trickery involved, for we usually expect definitions to be "serious." The humorous definition is a kind of joke on the listener or reader who, for a moment, finds something light or zany where he or she expected something serious or heavy.

Defining something gives us a kind of "power" and makes it possible to employ other techniques quite easily. Bierce's "bore" definition involves a kind of reversal (and a comment on human nature and our egoism and self-centeredness that is somewhat hostile). The "tree" definition relies on the technique of stereotyping—the woman driver who (since she's a woman) can't be expected to drive well and keeps on running into trees. Sexist material like this is now out of favor.

Disappointment and Defeated Expectations (logic)

> He: "Going to have dinner anywhere tonight?"
> She: (eagerly) "Why no, not that I know of."
> He: "You'll be awfully hungry."

Why did the chicken cross the road?
I don't know . . . why?
To get to the other side.

A schoolteacher was taking attendance. She came to a boy named Shakespeare. "And what's your first name," she asked? "William," replied the boy. "That's a pretty well known name, isn't it," she said. "Should be," replied to the boy. "I've lived here for ten years."

The technique of disappointment involves leading people on about something and then denying them the logical consequences they expect. It is very similar to teasing and is funny to the extent that we find minor disappointments amusing. A good deal depends on the frame or situation in which the disappointment is staged.

In *Informal Sociology*, William Bruce Cameron comes to the conclusion that jokes about sexual frustration are very common in America. He writes,

Mekeel and I concluded that one of the most striking features of sexual stories in our culture was the notion of personal deficiency. Most American sexual stories deal with in one way or another with sexual frustration. (1963, 90)

This probably has something to do with the power of American super-egos, which continually "triumph" over the id, though we also have many so-called "dirty jokes" in which sexual activity is consummated.

The aggression in these jokes comes from passivity, not activity; we expect a certain kind of response and don't get it. The technique of disappointment is the perfect one for people who might be characterized as "passive aggressive."

In the Shakespeare joke, it is the ignorance of the young boy that generates the humor; he has not heard of William Shakespeare and assumes that the name is well known because he has lived in the neighborhood for ten years.

Eccentricity (identity)

Mr. Smith: All doctors are quacks. And all patients, too. Only the Royal Navy is honest in England.
Mrs. Smith: But not sailors.
Mr. Smith: Naturally. [*A pause, still reading his paper*] Here's a thing I don't understand. In the newspaper they always give the age of deceased persons but never the age of newly born. That doesn't make sense.

MRS. SMITH: I never thought of that. [*Another moment of silence. The clock strikes three times. Silence. The clock doesn't strike.*]

MR. SMITH: [*Still reading his paper*] Tsk, it says here that Bobby Watson died.

MRS. SMITH: My God, the poor man! When did he die?

MR. SMITH: Why do you pretend to be astonished? You know very well that he's been dead these past two years. Surely you remember that we attended his funeral a year and a half ago.

(Eugene Ionesco, The Bald Soprano)

The humor of eccentricity is based on the difference between what is customary, "normal," or what we are used to and what we find when we experience the abnormal or the deviant. The humor of the absurd violates our sense of logic, our sense of the way humans think and behave. We can make a distinction between people who are strange (that is different, from foreign cultures) and people who are eccentric (who are from our culture and society and deviate from its norms). We might describe these people as "code violators." They do not live by our codes which, to us, seem quite reasonable and logical. In the right context, this code violation puzzles and amuses us.

In *The Bald Soprano*, everything is out of kilter. Mr. Smith wonders why the ages of deceased people are given but not of the newborn. On the face of it, in terms of the structure of the argument, there is a certain logic to his question. But it is absurd because in reality we know the age of all newborn children. And Bobby Watson died two years ago, Mr. Smith says, but his funeral wasn't held until a year and a half ago. Very weird behavior. Ionesco is obviously playing with logic and reason and creating characters who dispense with both of these matters.

Embarrassment—and Escape from It (identity)

> Ms. Jones lived on the second floor of an apartment building in Chicago. One morning she woke with a start when she heard the downstairs door open. She remembered she had forgotten to put out a milk bottle so she rushed to the kitchen, just as she was—al fresco—and stepped out across the hall. Suddenly she realized that it was too late to get back to the apartment so she slipped behind a door which closed on the water meters and waited for the milkman to depart. But it wasn't the milkman. It was the water inspector, who opened the door and found, to his surprise, Ms. Jones standing naked. "Oh, I'm sorry," she said. "I was expecting the milkman."

I've already said something about embarrassment in my discussion of coincidence, but there are a couple of additional points to be made.

Coincidences are often embarrassing, but as I suggested, one can have embarrassment without coincidences and coincidences without embarrassment. Saying a stupid thing or making some kind of an error can be embarrassing. In the sense the term is being used here, embarrassment involves being made uncomfortably self-conscious, ashamed and perhaps even confused.

We probably find embarrassment humorous because we feel superior to the person being embarrassed. This is because we are not the person being discomforted or humiliated. The joke about Ms. Jones involves mistakes (she thought she heard the milkman so she didn't bother getting dressed) and misunderstanding ("I was expecting the milkman," she says, which could be taken to mean that she had some kind of a tryst planned).

Exaggeration, Tall Tales, Comic Lies (language)

"When I was in India," said the club bore, "I saw a tiger come down to the water where some women were washing clothes. It was a very fierce tiger, but one woman, with great presence of mind, plashed some water in its face and it slunk away." Gentlemen," said a man in an armchair. "I can vouch for that story being true. A few minutes after that incident I met this tiger and stroked its whiskers. The whiskers were wet.

The mosquitos of Alaska are world famous for their size and ferocity. During the mosquito season no Alaskans go out at night, except in cars. One night, an unsuspecting visitor was seized by two gigantic mosquitos. "Shall we eat him here or take him to the swamp?" one of the mosquitos asked the other. "Here," said the other. "If we take him to the swamp, the big mosquitos will take him away from us."

Exaggeration in not necessarily humorous. As the examples above indicate, exaggeration must be tied to something else if it is to be seen as comic. In the first joke, we have a "bore," a traditional comic figure, whose story is "topped" by a second figure. This joke (or ones like it) is found in many joke books.

The second story is a classic tall tale. It is based upon a fantastic situation—asking listeners to believe that mosquitos can be large enough to seize human beings and then revealing that these mosquitos are relatively small ones. The tall tale involves exaggeration and ingenuity in finding ways of using exaggeration.

In both of these jokes, there is "topping." The tall tale establishes a "frame" that tells us that the exaggeration will be comic and that we can expect imagination and ingenuity as well as a touch of the absurd. Tall tales are comic lies that are based on the recognition of listeners that they are being lied to, so there is an element of paradox in this technique.

Exposure (identity)

> Dear John:
> Words cannot express how much I regret having broken off our engagement. Will you please come back to me? Your absence leaves a space no one can fill. Please forgive me and let us start over again. I can't live without you. I love you, love you, love you.
> Emily
> P.S. Congratulations on having won the Irish Sweepstakes.

There are several aspects of exposure as a humorous technique that should be considered. First, there can be exposure of stupidity or some other "hidden" quality of a person. If this "hidden" quality involves deception and is consciously kept from view, I see this as *unmasking* rather than exposure, per se, and deal with it elsewhere, as a separate technique. If what is hidden is merely not at the surface or is something a character in a humorous story is not aware of, it belongs under exposure. Unmasking also involves someone discovering something about someone else while exposure involves someone revealing something about himself or herself.

The second, and perhaps most important aspect of the humor of exposure involves obscenity and sexuality. Freud explains the humor of exposure (either physically or to obscene jokes) in his *Jokes and their Relation to the Unconscious* as follows:

> A chance exposure has a comic effect on us because we compare the ease with which we have enjoyed the sight with the great expenditure which would otherwise be required for reaching this end. (1963, 221–222)

This relates to his notion that we derive humor from an economy of effort in certain cases. In some cases, "mooning," when people drop their pants and reveal their rear ends in social situations, exposure has an aggressive and mildly hostile aspect to it.

In the joke above, Emily reveals she is a gold digger and, in addition, that she is too dumb to realize that she has revealed this. The incongruity between the romantic aspects of the letter and the mercenary nature of the postscript is also comic

Facetiousness (language)

> *A man was questioned about how it was that he had stayed married for thirty years without getting into an argument with his wife. "It was easy," the man said. "When we got married we decided that we would divide up spheres of responsibility. I make the big decisions and my wife makes the little ones. I decide when we go to war, raise taxes and how much to spend for foreign aid. My wife decides everything else.*

> *Falstaff:* Marry, then, sweet wag, when thou art king let not us that are squires of the night's body be called thieves of the day's beauty. Let us be Diana's foresters, gentlemen of the shade, minions of the moon; and let men say we be men of good government, being governed as the sea is, by our noble and chaste mistress the moon, under whose countenance we steal.

> (William Shakespeare, *Henry IV, Part One*, act 1, scene 2)

Facetiousness is generally taken to mean a joking, nonserious use of language. There is an element of ambiguity, for the person does not really mean (nor take seriously) what he or she says and this must be communicated one way or another. In the joke about the married couple, the man is revealing that his wife is the boss, though this is covered up by his assuming pseudoresponsibility for "important" decisions. And Falstaff is engaging in semantic obfuscation, as he suggests different ways of describing his profession—which is that of a robber. Facetiousness is similar to irony, but is weaker. In both techniques, we must "read" or "decode" the message; in irony there is a reversal, in facetiousness there is a discounting.

Grotesque (identity)

> Just then the sultry air coagulated and wove itself into the shape of a man—a transparent man of the strangest appearance. On his small head was a jockey cap, and he wore a short checked jacket fabricated of air. The man was seven feet tall but narrow in the shoulders, incredibly thin and with a face made for derision.

> (Michail Bulgakov, *The Master and the Margarita*)

> There was a young man of Devises
> Who had balls of two different sizes.
> One was so small

> It was no ball at all.
> The other so large it won prizes.

In the middle ages, there was a cruel delight in monstrous deformity and some of that may have carried over to the modern consciousness. The grotesque can be terrifying or it can be comic; in the latter case, it is probably because we maintain an element of psychological distance and sense of uninvolvement. This may be because some kind of a comic frame has been established which conditions the way we respond to grotesques: we escape the sense of terror that the grotesque can generate, via its fusion of incompatible elements into some crazy whole.

Thus, in the Bulgakov passage, we find a bizarre looking character whose difference from the norm makes him comic. The grotesque can also suggest characters who are so one-dimensional, so fixated on one thing, that they are seen as comic. We are back here to Bergson's notion of the mechanical being encrusted on the living. Humans are "flexible" and adaptable. When we find a lack of flexibility and monomania that can lead to all kinds of crazy situations, we find characters who can be seen as grotesque. They are not physically grotesque but psychologically (and perhaps spiritually) grotesque.

Ignorance, Gullibility, Naivete (logic)

> A little boy watched his mother smear herself with various gooey cosmetics. "What's that for, mummy?" he asked. "To make myself beautiful," she said, as she wiped off her face with a tissue. The boy eyed his mother. "Didn't work, did it."

> "Who killed Abel?" asked the circuit rider of a small boy in order to test his knowledge of the Bible. "I don't know nothing about it," answered the boy. "We just moved here two weeks ago." "Better watch him, parson," said an old-timer. "I ain't accusing him, but he looks mighty suspicious to me."

The humorous technique which involves ignorance, gullibility and naivete is closely related to the techniques of exposure and embarrassment. We gain a sense of superiority when the ignorance of others is revealed. We gain what Hobbes described as a feeling of "sudden glory arising from a sudden conception of some eminency in ourselves by comparison with the infirmity of others, or with our own formerly."

We have laughed at the ignorant, at the stupid, at fools (who are somewhat special in that they are often wise) for countless centuries. One thing fools and other stupid people do is help define other characters. We make sense of concepts and of people by contrasts, so stupid people, fools, dummies, etc. play a role in helping so-called serious characters establish or define themselves. There may also be a kind of pleasure from regression, since we were, once, "dumb" and "stupid," when we were very young, naive, and gullible. Perhaps these characters enable us to regress, momentarily and pleasurably, to our childhoods.

In the first joke, the little boy tells what he thinks, which is one of the failings of the young. He hasn't learned to be polite and avoid unwittingly insulting his mother. In the second joke, both the young boy and the old timer are revealed as ignorant, neither one knowing the story of Cain and Abel. The young are often a source of amusement since they often reveal things (not recognizing what they are doing) that their parents or others don't want to be made public.

Imitation and Pretense (identity)

> Mrs. Doyle was furious. She rolled a newspaper into a club and struck her husband with it. He surprised her by playing the fool. He growled like a dog and caught the paper in his teeth. When she let go of her end, he dropped to his hands and knees and continued the imitation on the floor.

> (Nathanael West, *Miss Lonelyhearts*)

VOLPONE
> Loving Mosca! (Looking into a mirror.)
> 'Tis well. My pillow now, and let him enter. (Exit Mosca.)
> Now, my feigned cough, my phthisic, and my gout,
> My apoplexy, palsy, and catarrhs,
> Help with your forced functions, this my posture Wherein, this three year, I have mocked their hopes. He comes, I hear him—-uh! uhF! uh! uh! O—
> (Ben Jonson, *Volpone*, act 1, scene 2)

A distinction can be made between *imitation*, which involves things and states of being, and *impersonation*, which involves assuming an identity (of a person, someone in a profession, etc.). In imitation, a person pretends he or she is something else—a dog or other animal or a machine, for instance—but maintains his or her identity, which is fused with that which is imitated. In impersonation, a person takes on a different identity.

Both imitation and impersonation can be distinguished from *mimicry*, in which a person maintains his own identity but takes on that of some familiar person. In imitation, the humor stems from the difference between the thing being imitated and the persona and nature of the imitator. A human pretending to be a dog can be funny and so can a dog pretending to be a human, as in the case of Snoopy and various other "humanized" or anthropomorphized animals. Incongruity seems to be at work here, though often we find other phenomena as well. In pretense, a person imitates a different state of being, as in the case where Volpone pretends to be a dying man. In imitation there is no conscious attempt to deceive, while pretense does involve deception. When we push the deception further, we arrive at impersonation, in which a person takes on a different identity.

Impersonation and Recognition (identity)

Impersonation is one of the more direct forms of the humor of identity. In impersonation an individual's identity is "stolen" from him and usually submitted to various forms of comic degradation. The degradations and the confusions usually associated with the impersonation (frequently tied to the comedy of errors) are often funny. In addition, there is a tension established: will the person being impersonated get his identity back, will the impersonator be discovered? And what happens to the people who have been fooled by the impersonation?

There is also impersonation of professions. Here an individual pretends to be some kind of a professional and, as such, steals an occupational identity, not an individual one. The incongruity between the actual qualifications of the impersonator and his pretended ones, and the way people react to him because of his appropriated qualifications and status, generates much of the humor here. This kind of humor provides an ironic commentary on human nature. It shows that we judge people, too often, not on the basis of what they are and on their obvious personal characteristics but on the basis of their status and what it is assumed they must be like. Thus, impersonators make fools of the people they entertain in the same way that they often make fools of the persons they pretend to be.

Sometimes this process is involuntary. A person makes a mistake, does not realize that he is impersonating someone (a high official, for instance) and rather fantastic consequences result. There is an old story by Sholem Aleichem called "The Hat" that tells of an old Jew at a railroad station unknowingly putting on the wrong hat (that of a high government official) and being treated by everyone with great deference. And Gogol's *Inspector General* is based on someone being mistaken for an inspector general, with all kinds of hilarious consequences.

Infantilism (language)

MRS. SMITH: Mice have lice, lice haven't mice.
MRS. MARTIN: Don't ruche my brooch!
MRS. MARTIN: Don't smooch the brooch!
MRS. SMITH: Groom the goose, don't goose the groom.

(Ionesco, *The Bald Soprano*)

Freud traces jokes back to playing with words and "thoughts which have been frustrated by rational criticism." It seems likely that children experience pleasure in manipulating sounds when they are very young, and words when older. This leads to a relatively simple kind of humor and though it has possibilities for ingenious manipulation, as the Ionesco citation demonstrates, its uses are limited. Puns also rely on sound play, but the good puns also involve meaning. When adults indulge in infantile forms of humor (as they do when singing songs such as "Mersey Dotes") it probably reflects a momentary regression in the service of the ego.

Insults (language)

I can but wonder what will become of the *Times* editor when the breath leaves his feculent body and death stops the rattling of his abortive brain, for he is unfit for heaven and too foul for hell. He cannot be buried in the earth lest he provoke a pestilence, nor in the sea lest he poison the fish, nor swung into space like Mahomet's coffin lest the circling worlds, in trying to avoid contamination, crash together, wreck the universe and bring again the noisome reign of Chaos and old Night.

(W.C. Brann, *The Iconoclast*)

PRINCE: I'll be no longer guilty of this sin. This sanguine coward, this bed-presser, this
        horseback breaker, this huge hill of flesh . . .
FALSTAFF: 'Sblood, you starveling, you eel-skin, you dried neat's tongue, you bull's
        pizzle, you stockfish! O for breath to utter what is like thee! You tailor's yard, you
        sheath, you bowcase, you standing tuck.

(William Shakespeare, *Henry IV Part One*, act 2, scene 4)

Although most of the techniques of humor involve what we might describe as "masked aggression and hostility," in the technique known as insults, these submerged feelings are made obvious. It may be that audience members or readers of insults get double benefits: first, they can "collaborate" in the aggression and gain pleasure from this collaboration; second, they are not actively involved in it, and need not feel guilty about it.

Insults, by themselves, are not seen as funny; there has to be a comic play frame established and there have to be other techniques involved, such as comparisons, exaggeration, ridicule, etc. We do not feel as guilty about humorous insults as we do about ordinary ones because our ids can tell our superegos that "we were only fooling." And trading insults, repartee, spreads any blame that might occur to all the parties involved.

Irony (language)

> The king condescended to visit a surgical clinic and came on the professor as he was carrying out the amputation of a leg. He accompanied all its stages with loud expressions of his royal satisfaction. "Bravo! Bravo! My Dear Professor!" When the operation was finished, the professor approached him and asked him, with a deep bow, "Is it your Majesty's command that I should remove the other leg, too?"
>
> (Quoted by Sigmund Freud in *Jokes and Their Relation to the Unconscious*.)
>
> *A Jewish man named Katzman decided to change his name to a French name so people wouldn't be able to recognize he was Jewish. He went to a Judge for help. "French, you say," said the Judge. "Well, the French word for cat is chat and the French word for man is l'homme. We will change your name to Chat-l'homme."*

The humor in irony stems from the gap that exists between what is said and what is meant. There are a number of kinds of irony. The first, known as Socratic irony, involves the pretence of ignorance to make another person's false ideas become obvious. This is done by adroit or judicious questioning. The other kind of irony involves saying something but meaning the opposite. This is what we usually understand as irony. There is another kind, known as dramatic irony (or tragic irony) which involves characters believing in the opposite of what is the truth of a given situation or acting in a way that leads to the opposite of their desires taking place.

One problem with irony is that the intention of the ironist must be made clear; that is, people must realize that someone means the opposite of what he or she says. Sometimes people don't "get" the irony, and take what was said ironically in a literal way. So it is a dangerous method of generating humor. One has to develop a character who is ironic and set the stage for our interpreting this character's ironic comments as ironic. The irony in the joke about Katzman changing his name to something "French sounding" is that his name ends up even more Jewish, as the Hebrew word "shalom" which means "hello."

Literalness (language)

> A killer was facing trial and feared for his life. He got one of his friends to bribe one of the jury members who seemed stupid enough to take a bit of advice. The friend told the juror to "hold out for manslaughter." The trial went on and jury went out for deliberations, which lasted days and days. Finally the jury came in with a verdict of manslaughter. "Good work," said the gangster's friend, "but what took you so long?" "It was a hard fight," said the juror. "Everyone else wanted to acquit him.

> A man walked into a clothing store. "What can I do for you?" asked a clerk. "I'd like to try on that suit in the window," said the man. "We'd rather have you use the dressing room."

> Why did the moron take a ladder to the party?
> He heard the drinks were on the house.

The humor of literalness (or more precisely overliteralness) is based on the inability of some character to take circumstances into account and interpret a request in a reasonable manner. This is basic. There is also the matter of stupidity (overliteralness and being a moron) and misunderstanding (taking a figurative statement literally). It is the mechanicalness of the behavior that generates the humor. Bergson defines laughter as "*something mechanical encrusted on the living*" and adds, later, "a comic effect is obtained whenever we pretend to take literally an expression which was used figuratively."

Mimicry (identity)

PRINCE: I am not yet of Percy's mind, the Hotspur of the North, he that kills me some six or seven Scots at a breakfast, washes his hands, and says to his wife, "Fie upon this quiet life! I want work." "O my sweet Harry," says she, "how many hast thou killed to-day?" "Give my roan horse a drench," says he, and answers, "some fourteen," an hour later, "a trifle, a trifle." I prithee call in Falstaff. I'll play Percy,

and that damned brawn shall play Dame Mortimer his wife. "Rivo!" says the
drunkard. "Call in ribs, call in tallow."

(William Shakespeare, *Henry IV Part One*, act 2, scene 4)

Mimicry is a form of humor which involves a person maintaining his
own identity while, at the same time, "stealing" or "borrowing" the
identity of others. The entertainers we call impersonators are really
mimics, for they don't impersonate Cary Grant or Marlon Brando or
some politician as much as mimic them. The humor stems from having
someone else's voice, mannerisms, and personality coming from an
obviously incorrect source. The appropriation of these matters by the
mimic is another example of incongruity.

Mimics do not settle for voice imitations alone. The mimics must use
other techniques (allusions to embarrassing events, ridicule, exaggeration, insults, revelations of stupidity, etc.) to generate humor. In order to
be mimicked, a person must be well known (so we can compare the
mimic and the "real thing") and have a highly personal and individualistic
"presence," style of speaking or singing, etc. In some cases, such as Rich
Little's mimicking of Richard Nixon, Little could make himself look like
Nixon and sound like Nixon and also use the same body language as
Nixon.

Mistakes (logic)

> *A cowboy was riding one day when he saw a snake. He pulled out a gun and was
> about to shoot it when a fairy appeared and pleaded for the snake's life. She said it
> was her favorite snake and that if he spared it she would grant him any wish he made.
> He spared the snake and asked to be made the handsomest man in the world. When
> he returned home that night he looked in the mirror and sure enough, he was the
> handsomest man in the world. A month later he saw the same snake and was just
> about to shoot it when the fairy appeared and promised him one more wish if he would
> spare the snake. "You've made me so irresistable that I need the genitals of this horse
> in order to satisfy all the women that will want me." The fairy looked at him curiously.
> "I'll shoot the snake if you don't grant my wish." "If you insist," said the fairy." When
> the cowboy got home, he happened to glance at himself in the mirror and was amazed.
> He had been riding Sally.*

Mistakes lead to what we know as the the comedy of errors. Mistakes
are based on some kind of error, inattention, poor judgement, or ignorance. (Misunderstandings, on the other hand, are verbal and involve

intellectual error.) We laugh at the momentary inadequacy of the person making the mistake, at his or her lack of knowledge. This makes us feel superior to the person making the mistake.

In the cowboy joke, the cowboy "outwitted" himself. In some cases, such as *A Comedy of Errors*, we have identical twins, so there is reason for the characters to make mistakes. These mistakes lead to all kinds of complications. Mistakes by themselves are not funny; it is only when the comic frame is in place and the mistakes lead to slapstick, embarrassments, revelations of ignorance (or of other kinds), comic insults and the like that we find mistakes funny.

Misunderstanding (language)

> *The Duke of Marlborough was once given an emu. It was sent to his estate and created great interest since there was a chance it would procreate. Eventually, while the Duke and Dutchess were on a trip, it laid an egg. The housekeeper sent a telegram informing of the event that went as follows— "Emu had laid egg; in the absence of your grace, have put a goose on it."*

> *In Minnesota every other person is named Olson. One day, two Olsons went to a judge to be married. The judge turned to the male: Name Please? "John Olson. They call me Ollie." The judge then turned to the bride-to be. Your name please? "Mary Olson." Relations? asked the judge? "Only once," said Mary, blushing. "Ollie couldn't wait."*

Misunderstanding is, as has been pointed out already, a verbal matter that is tied, frequently, to the ambiguity of language or the strange meanings language generates when taken out of context. It is this ambiguity, of course, which also gives language its power. In the Duke of Marlborough joke, the telegram seems to suggest that since the Duke was not available to sit on the egg, a goose was put on it, instead. The phrase "in the absence of your grace" was meant to convey, "since you were not here to tell us what to do," but doesn't convey that information. In the same way, when the judge asked Mary Olson about "relations," he was inquiring whether they were related to one another, not whether they had had sexual relations.

One of the most famous examples of misunderstanding is found in the Abbott and Costello routine about "who's on first." In this routine, baseball players on a team have unusual names like Who, What, etc. Abbott tries to explain this to Costello, who misunderstands things and does not realize that Who is the name of the first baseman, not a question about the name of the person playing first base.

Parody (identity)

> *Philosophy I:* Everyone from Plato to Camus is read. The following topics are covered: Ethics: The categorical imperative and six ways to make it work for you. Aesthetics: Is art the mirror of life, or what? . . . Epistemology: Is knowledge knowable? If not, how do we know this? The Absurd: Why existence is often considered silly, particularly for men who wear brown and white shoes. Manyness and oneness are studied as they relate to otherness. (Students achieving oneness will move ahead to twoness.)

> (Woody Allen, "Spring Bulletin")

Parody is a form of verbal mimicry or imitation in which the style and mannerisms of some well-known writer are ridiculed. In order for parody to be effective, the writer being parodied must be well known and have a distinctive way of writing. It is also possible to parody a famous work, a genre, or a style of writing. The selection by Woody Allen parodies the style of writing found in college bulletins.

In addition to imitating style, there should be other comic techniques employed to heighten the humor. In the numerous parodies of Hemingway, his use of language and his typical characters are ridiculed. In parodying a James Bond spy novel, various distinctive features of these works must be dealt with: M sending Bond on a mission, Q giving Bond bizarre weapons, Bond having his drinks shaken and not stirred, Bond making love to exotic women, Bond being captured and tortured (generally) by some powerful male villain, Bond defeating/killing the villain, etc. Thus, we must ridicule what is distinctive in a work.

Parody is probably one of the most powerful and commonly used technique for generating humor and some theorists of comedy claim that all humor stems from parody.

Puns, Word Play, and Other Amalgamations (language)

> *An English wit couldn't help himself, but made puns on all occasions. On being taken to an orphan asylum he said, "This far and no father." The next morning, at breakfast, he declared, as he bit into a roll, "The bun is the lowest form of wheat." Finally his friends thought they'd silence him by taking him to see the Grand Canyon. He gazed at it for a while. "Gorge-ous, isn't it?"*

The pun is frequently called, as the joke above reminds us, "the lowest form of wit." This is not correct, for some puns are very clever. It is the bad puns, which play on language in too forced or obvious a manner, that elicit our groans. In a good pun, there is a play on meaning; in a bad pun, there is only a play on sound.

From a semiotic perspective, a pun can be seen to be a signifier that stands for two signifieds. A signifier is defined as anything that can be used to stand for something else. Typically, a signifier is a sound (or word) or object. A signified is a concept or that which is signified. Thus, in the joke above, the term *father* can mean either parent of a child (a father) or distance (I won't go any farther). When the punster says "no father" he means he won't walk farther but the phrase also applies to orphans, who have no fathers.

We seem to enjoy playing with language, and puns, as well as other examples such as neologisms and amalgamations (such as "cinemactor," an amalgamation of cinema and actor) give us pleasure, probably as a result of what Freud described as "an economy of expenditure." We use one word but it has two meanings.

Repartee and Outwitting (language)

> There is a story told about a meeting between Noel Coward and an actress, Lady Diana Manners, who encountered one another at a party. Neither liked the other.
> "Did you see my play, Private Lives, asked Mr. Coward.
> "Yes," replied the actress.
> "What did you think of it?" asked Coward.
> "Not very amusing," replied Lady Diana.
> "Did you see me play the virgin in The Miracle?" asked Lady Diana.
> "Yes," replied Coward.
> "What did you think of it?" she asked.
> "Very amusing," replied Coward.

> Isadora Duncan is reputed to have written to George Bernard Shaw suggesting they breed together in the interests of eugenics. "Just imagine," she supposedly wrote, "of a child with my body and your brains." "Yes, madam, but what of a child with my body and your brains?" Shaw supposedly replied.

Repartee is a technique which counters aggression with aggression. It is a form of verbal dueling in which the game is to rebut an insult with a better insult. Time is of importance, for the repartee must be made immediately, suggesting that repartee is intimately connected with wit.

Frequently we think of witty and amusing replies we should have made to comments when it is too late to make them.

We laugh at repartee because we delight in seeing the determined defense of the ego by a person and the eventual embarrassment of a would-be aggressor, whose id suddenly finds itself attacked. Repartee involves insult, a standard technique of humor. Repartee also is a form of verbal outwitting, very similar to what we see in chase scenes or in a technique involving embarrassment and escape from it.

Repetition and Pattern (logic)

> *A hunter's car broke down in the midst of a lonely stretch of country. After walking a few miles he found a log cabin in the woods in which a settler and his wife and three children lived.*
>
> *The hunter was fed very well and started feeling drowsy. The settler asked him to stay with them and the hunter accepted. "You'll have to wait a bit while I put the children to bed," said the settler. They were all put to bed and when the last one was asleep the settler gently lifted them, one by one, and laid them on the floor in the back of the room. "She's all yours now," said the settler. The hunter protested but was persuaded. Due to his exhaustion he fell immediately into a deep sleep. When he woke up he was also on the floor with the kids, and the settler and his wife were in the bed.*

Repetition is a technique of humor that is found in many places. It is part of theme-and-variations and the humor of before and after, in addition to having its own identity. The humor of repetition comes from the tension created by some kind of a series being established. We wonder whether the series will be able to maintain itself or whether some interesting variation will take place?

In *Anatomy of Criticism*, Northrop Frye explains how repetition can be used by the humorists and argues that it informs our most significant humor. He writes,

> The principle of humor is the principle of unincremental repetition. The literary imitation of ritual bondage is funny. . . . Repetition overdone or not going anywhere belongs to comedy, for laughter is partly a reflex, and like other reflexes, it can be conditioned by a simple repeated pattern.
>
> The principle of repetition as the basis of humor both in Jonson's sense and in ours is well-known to the creators of comic-strips, in which a character is established as a parasite or glutton (often confined to one dish), or a shrew, and who begins to be funny after the point has been made every day for several months. Continuous comic radio programs, too, are much more amusing to habitues than to neophytes. (1967,168)

Comedy is peopled by eccentrics, grotesques, monomaniacs of one sort or another, who persist in their behavior no matter what situation they find themselves in. Their unwillingness or inability to "bend" or to take changed circumstances into account strikes us as amusing. This kind of behavior is what Bergson called "mechanical." We probably find these characters amusing (and repetition, itself amusing) because we feel superior to them. We would, we tell ourselves, be much more rational and reasonable.

Reversal and Contradiction (logic)

An Edible: Good to eat and wholesome to digest, as a worm to a toad, a toad to a snake, a snake to a pig, a pig to a man, and a man to a worm.

(Ambrose Bierce, *The Devil's Dictionary*)

A woman boarded a bus and sat down next to a middle-aged man reading a newspaper. After the bus had started she nudged the man and said, "Tell me, are you Jewish?" "No, I'm not," he replied. Ten minutes later she nudged him again. "You don't have to be ashamed . . . tell me, are you Jewish?" "I'm sorry, I'm not," he answered in an irritated voice. Ten minutes later she nudged him again. "Are you sure you're not Jewish?" The man got tired of her bothering him and decided to humor her. "Yes," he said, "I'm Jewish." "Funny," she replied, "You don't look Jewish."

Reversal is one of the more common devices used to create humor. Reversal reveals the absurd elements in life and offers insights that are amusing and sometimes profound. Reversal is very similar to what has been called "dramatic irony," which involves a resolution of some action that turns out to be the opposite of what is hoped for.

In the *Edible* selection, we have a comic definition that is based on the notion of reversal in that worms start out being eaten and end up eating in the great cycle of life, as Bierce describes it. Reversal also is similar to repartee except that reversal doesn't involve insults.

Ridicule (language)

You dedicate yourself to the pursuit of pleasure. No overindulgence, mind you, but knowing that your body is a pleasure machine you treat it carefully to get the most out of it. Golf as well as booze, Philadelphia Jack O'Brien and his chestweights as well as Spanish dancers. Nor do you neglect the pleasures of the mind. You fornicate under pictures by Matisse and Picasso, you drink from Renaissance glassware, and often you spend an evening beside the fireplace with Proust and an apple . . .

(Nathanael West, *Miss Lonelyhearts*)

Ridicule is a form of direct verbal attack against a person, thing, or idea. It is designed to cause contemptuous laughter and humiliation, though in some cases ridicule is fairly genial. Ridicule takes a number of forms: *deriding*, which involves attacking someone with a scornful tone; *mocking*, which is to imitate another's appearance or actions; and *taunting*, which is to remind someone of some annoying fact.

In the West selection, the life of the aesthete is ridiculed in a display of rhetorical brilliance. West plays different aspects of culture off against one another—Picasso and fornication, booze and Renaissance glassware—and derides the romantic "pretensions" of literary types who think it glorious to spend an evening with Proust and an apple.

Rigidity (logic)

> *A man was waiting for a friend at a fashionable club. Having arrived somewhat early, he decided to pass the time playing billiards and asked an elderly gentlemen sitting near him whether he would care to play billiards. "No," replied the man. "Tried it once and didn't like it." "Perhaps you would care for a game of cards," he asked the elderly gentleman. "No," replied the elderly gentleman. "Tried it once and didn't like it. Besides, my son will be arriving soon." "Your only son, I presume," said the man.*

Rigidity is a form of over literalness, except that rigidity involves actions and behavior rather than a simple-minded interpretation of language. The rigid person is a grotesque of sorts, a "mechanical" man or woman whose single-mindedness becomes a source of laughter. It is this inability to react to circumstances, this stiffness, this single-mindedness that amuses us. Rigidity suggests a diminished consciousness, a lack of intelligence; we feel superior to those who are so rigid that they create absurd situations for themselves and others.

Much comedy involves rigid types of characters who are locked into their roles as impostors, buffoons, braggarts, cowards, and so on. Rigidity is one of the bases of Commedia Dell'Arte, with its cast of personalities who always play certain roles, and much contemporary comedy, which pits various "types" of characters against one another in television sitcoms and other serial comic forms.

Sarcasm (language)

A woman's car stalled at a corner and remained there while the light turned red, yellow and green several times. Finally a traffic cop came up to her and said, "What's the matter, lady? Don't we have any colors you like?"

Sarcasm stems from the Greek *sarkazein*, "to tear the flesh, to bite." It involves the use of cutting, contemptuous, and "biting" remarks, delivered often in a hostile manner. The manner of delivery is often very important, for the tone must be such that we recognize that someone is attacking someone else and making a sarcastic remark. Some people use sarcasm as a stance, as an everyday manner of dealing with people; it does not lead to winning friends and influencing people. Sarcasm may generate some humor but it tends to be a costly kind of humor, unless the sarcasm is directed towards oneself and turned into a form of victim humor.

Satire (language)

A man so various that he seemed to be
Not one, but all mankind's epitome:
Stiff in opinions, always in the wrong
Was everything by starts and nothing long;
But in the course of one revolving moon
Was chemist, statesman, fiddler, and buffoon;
Then all for women, painting, rhyming, drinking
Besides ten thousand freaks that died in thinking.

(John Dryden, "Absalom and Achitophel")

Satire is one of the most important literary forms of humor and has been used by writers and engaged the attention of scholars and critics for thousands of years. Generally it attacks the status quo, and can be seen as a force for resistance, though this isn't always the case. (Some satirists attack those who are critical of the status quo, but satire generally pokes fun at those in power.) Satire is a rather general technique of humor that makes use of many of the techniques discussed in this glossary: ridicule, exaggeration, insult, (invidious) comparison, and so on. Generally speaking, satirists attack specific individuals or institutions or happenings. We talk about humorists—whether they be standup comedians, comic strip artists, writers, or film makers—satirizing someone or something, so I think it is fair to consider satire to be a technique of humor.

In his *Anatomy of Criticism*, Northrop Frye (1957, 224) suggests there are a number of kinds of satire: *Horatian satire*, which attacks foibles and folly in a genial manner; *Juvenalian satire*, which is savage in its condemnation of error and misbehavior; and *Menippean satire*. This latter form,

> deals less with people as such than with mental attitudes. Pedants, bigots, cranks, parvenus, virtuosi, enthusiasts, rapacious and incompetent professional men of all kinds, are handled in terms of their occupational approach to life as distinct from their social behavior.

This kind of satire focuses upon roles people play and deals with "rigid" types of people, as discussed above. The satirist is critical and implies that the social order need not be as it is and that many people (in the professions and in positions of power) are really fools and cranks.

The Dryden quotation is an attack on the Duke of Buckingman that is full of insults, all done in beautiful rhyme. The Duke is attacked for being "stiff in opinion" (rigid), "always in the wrong" (stupid) and many other things. Satire is often moral (and by implication, political) but it is often directly political as well, as the comic strip *Doonesbury* shows so brilliantly.

Scale (identity)

> The eyes of Doctor T.J. Eckleburg are blue and gigantic—their retinas are one yard high. They look out from no face, but, instead, from a pair of enormous yellow spectacles which pass over a non-existent nose.
>
> (F. Scott Fitzgerald, *The Great Gatsby*)

Large-sized objects or very small ones often create humor through their incongruity. Scale can also be used to defeat expectations. We expect something "normal" size (a steak) and get something "unusual" (a tiny little steak or a gigantic steak). Scale indirectly reduces or enlarges the sense spectators have of themselves (as they identify with a character in a film or book, for example) and that generates a strange feeling which has a humorous element to it. Putting us next to a giant has the effect of turning us into midgets or children and this is a shock to our sense of self and achieved identities. The reverse happens when we become giants. Swift used scale in *Gulliver's Travels* brilliantly.

In *Easy Street*, Charlie Chaplin finds himself up against a gigantic tough, who throws cops around as if they are stuffed animals. We empathize and identify with Chaplin as he fights and subdues this villain, turning him into a good Churchgoer. Could there be an element of the Oedipal struggle reflected in battles between small heroes and big villains? Is scale a reminder of the battles we all waged (if Freud was right about the Oedipus Complex) before we turned our attention to other things?

There is an element of resistance in comedy involving scale, a sense that smaller, weaker elements can actually prevail (if ingenious and bold enough) over more powerful forces. It may even be that political resistance, as we understand the term, is connected to those who have survived their Oedipal struggles without being devastated, without abandoning a sense of resistance to the powers that be.

Slapstick (action, nonverbal)

Slapstick is physical humor, often involving degradation by action. The throwing of a pie in the face of a person is an externalized, objectified form of an insult. It works by taking a person who claims an adult status (and, perhaps, a position of authority) and turning him into (someone resembling) a babbling infant, who makes messes when he eats. It is a somehow infantile form of humor both as far as the pie thrower (the baby who throws his food around) and the pie receiver (the baby who makes messes when he eats).

Slapstick involves all kinds of physical actions that amuse us—slipping on bananas, sliding around on greasy floors, getting pies in the face, being hit with mops, etc. It is an "attack" on our claims to adulthood, importance, and status of any kind. As such, it feeds on an inner sense of egalitarianism we have, a feeling that all claims to superiority are invalid. Slapstick is a kind of "democratic" degradation that is tied to a sense we have that we are all humans and the similarities between people are more important than the artificial differences created by social institutions.

Speed (action, nonverbal)

Speed is not intrinsically funny. Automobile races, for example, are not seen as humorous. But speed can be turned into something funny, as in chase scenes, where the action is speeded up and the pursuers and the pursued are made to run at incredible speeds. Why we see something like this as funny is difficult to say. Perhaps rapid speed (or the opposite, slow motion) attacks our sense of adulthood and rationality, our feeling that we understand how the world functions. There is an incongruous element introduced that strikes us as uncanny and amusing.

There is also an element of animal exuberance to speed. We are delighted when we see individuals "defying" the laws of nature, refusing to be bound by them. We feel that we, too, can resist certain forces in society that pass themselves off as immutable and all powerful. We frequently find speed in chase scenes, where we identify with the attempts of a comic figure to escape from being caught, which would entail being punished, also. As Chaplin runs, pursued by all kinds of villains, we run with him and as he turns on the speed, we feel a sense of exhilaration.

In some comedy commercials, we find people who can speak incredibly quickly and this strikes us as very amusing. When they speak this fast, it almost sounds like doubletalk and gibberish, yet we can identify the words. We find these commercials comic because the speed of the talking is so remarkable. This fast-talking becomes a kind of feat.

Stereotype and Stock Type (identity)

> *Three Scotchmen were in church one morning when the minister made a strong appeal for some very worthy cause and asked everyone in the congregation to give at least six shillings. The three Scots became very nervous as the collection neared them. When it got to their row, one of them fainted and the other two carried him out.*
>
> *What has an IQ of 350?*
> *Poland.*

Jokes involving stereotypes can be described as generalized insults— attacks on races, religions, ethnic groups, etc. but there is more to the humor of stereotypes than that. Stereotypes are useful to writers and comedians because they are instant (pseudo) "explanations" of behavior and they enable people to understand "motivation." Thus, Scots are stereotyped as cheap and if you find a Scot in a joke, he or she will probably be cheap.

Stereotypes are, from a sociological point of view, group-held notions people have about other groups. Stereotypes can be negative, positive, or mixed, but in all cases they are extreme over-simplifications and generalizations. And most of the time they are very harmful and insulting. Thus, Polish people are stereotyped as dumb, Italians as dirty or cowardly, Jews as materialistic, English as snobs, and so on. Stereotypes vary from culture to culture; in England, for example, it is the Irish who are stereotyped as dumb, not Polish people. The mechanism behind stereotypes is insult and an ensuing sense of superiority on the part of those using stereotypes.

Stock types are somewhat different. They go back to antiquity and deal not with ethnic or religious types but personality types. As Northrop Frye writes,

> The *Tractatus* lists three types of comic characters: the *alazons* or impostors, the *eirons* or self-deprecators, and the buffoons (bomolochoi). This list is closely related to a passage in the Ethics which contrasts the first two, and then goes on to contrast the buffoon with a character whom Aristotle calls *agroikos* or churlish, literally rustic. We may reasonably accept the churl as a fourth character type, and so we have two opposed pairs. The contest of the *eiron* and *alazon* forms the basis of the comic action, and the buffoon and churl polarize the comic mood. (1957, 172)

A good number of our important comedians, humorists, and writers of humor either identify themselves as one of the above or make use of these (and other) stock types and stereotypes.

Theme and Variation (logic)

> An American professor met three members of the Academie Francaise in Paris and asked them for their definition of savoir-faire. "This is not difficult," said one of the members. "If I go home and find my wife kissing another man and I tip my hat to them and say 'excuse me,' that is savoir-faire." "No, not really," said the second. If I go home and find my wife kissing another man and I say 'continue,' that is savoir-faire." "No, not yet," said the third. "If I go home and find my wife kissing another man and tip my hat and say 'excuse me, but please continue,' and he can continue . . . he has savoir-faire."

> An Irishman was digging a ditch in a notorious red light district when he noticed a Protestant minister entering one of the houses of ill repute. "So what I've heard is true," he thought. Then he notices a rabbi entering the house. "Six of one, half a

dozen of another," he thought. Then he saw a priest enter the house. "Must be someone sick in there," he thought.

The use of variations on a theme is a technique that makes its basic appeal to logic and the understanding. The technique shows the relativity of things, and focuses on how different people, members of groups, cultures, etc. go about doing things. Implicit in theme and variation humor is the notion that we live in a complex world full of people with different values and beliefs. This technique must be used in conjunction with other techniques, such as stereotyping, stock types, insult, and exaggeration to be effective.

Peter Ustinov wrote a play, *The Love of Four Colonels*, which used theme and variation very effectively. In the play four colonels, from the United States, France, England and Russia, attempt to seduce a beautiful young woman—each in his "national manner." Ustinov dealt with stereotypes of national character in the play; it was about stereotypes and very similar, in structure, to the joke about savoire-faire. This technique is found in humor about groups of various kinds that differ in various respects: Americans, Russians and Frenchmen, or priests, ministers and rabbis, as the joke above demonstrates.

Unmasking and Revelation of Character (identity)

A handsome young businessman stationed in Tokyo came to America on a trip where he met a lovely young girl who he courted and married. "You'll love Tokyo," he told the girl. "I have a servant, Yamaka, who does everything. We'll have a wonderful time." When they arrived in Tokyo, the young man introduced the girl to Yamaka, who bowed and retired. The next morning, the young man said to his wife, "I have to go to the office, but you can continue to sleep . . . don't worry . . . Yamaka will take care of everything." Several hours later the young wife was nudged gently by the servant. "Okay, missee . . . time to go home now."

I have dealt with the theme of unmasking earlier, in my discussion of impersonation, imitation, and mimicry but I would like to distinguish between these forms and unmasking, in general. The emphasis in unmasking is on the process and effects of discovery, while in the other techniques it is on the pretense. In unmasking, what is revealed or discovered often leads to embarrassment and humiliation. There is a tension established between the the "mask" and what is revealed by the unmasking process.

With this, my discussion of the basic techniques of humor comes to a conclusion. In many cases we find techniques complementing one another to generate humor; sometimes a technique, by itself, is not necessarily funny. When a number of techniques combine with one another, the effect is often more than the sum of the parts. These techniques enable us to "anatomize" humor, to find out what it is, in any example of humor, that generates laughter, mirth or whatever. I do not believe that humorists have these techniques in mind when they create humor. But they use these techniques, in various permutations and combinations, based, in large part, on their experiences, their memories about "what worked" in earlier books, performances, and so on.

Not only can we find out what techniques are found in a given work, we can also see how an author or performer has evolved as a creative artist. We can also see whether certain techniques tend to be popular at certain periods, which enables us to gain valuable insights about the forces of resistance and control that were operating. This glossary is the only work I know of which deals with the techniques of humor found in all kinds of humor; other works deal with forms of humor (the joke, the limerick, the satire) and with "why" theories of humor. This glossary might be amended with additional techniques that can be used to generate humor, but despite its limitations and imperfections, it is still a useful tool for humor researchers and creators.

2

Anatomy of a Joke

Jokes, as I've already suggested, are not the best way to be funny but they are a common form of humor and, as such, deserve some attention. We tell jokes to amuse people, to generate laughter. This laughter is a response to messages we have been given about relationships among people, places, and things. Laughter is a response to information—but a special kind—which is based, so different theorists suggest, on incongruities, masked aggression, a feeling of superiority, or things such as signs and play frames.

Incongruity is generally defined as involving a lack of harmony, something that is inconsistent or improper—or, in very general terms, involving shifts of one kind or another. If we think of incongruity this way we can use paired bipolar oppositions to characterize some of the more common approaches to laughter and humor.

Theories of Humor as Oppositions

In the chart that follows I will list some of these theories or approaches in terms of paired or bipolar oppositions that are found in them.

Theorists	Bipolar Opposition
Hobbes	Superior/Inferior Attitude
Freud	Conscious/Unconscious Aggression
Bergson	Mechanical/Flexible Behavior
Bateson	Lies/Truth Paradox (self-contradiction)
Fry	Real/Unreal Frames
Berger	Violate/Maintain Codes

57

I have suggested that it is profitable to look at jokes in terms of the codes they maintain and violate and this violation can be seen as based on some kind of incongruity in relationships that is characterized by people as "humorous" which means, among other things, not serious.

The Structure of a Joke

If we look at a joke structurally we find the following:

Jokemes. They are minimal elements of the joke such as actions undertaken by individuals, or things said.

Relationships. The joke establishes relationships among the individuals in the joke or makes reference to the experiences of listeners and their relationships with others.

Laughter. The response to the telling of the joke and the establishment of relationships that are suddenly and unexpectedly (incongruously) altered by the punch line. From the perspective being discussed, there is generally some kind of violation of a code that is involved in the joke.

The codes upon which the jokes are based must be known and explicit. In some cultures, mothers-in-law or old people or certain animals have high status and are not seen as the proper subject of humor. Thus, jokes told by Americans about mothers-in-law or old people would not be amusing. And jokes about these subjects that were acceptable thirty years ago would not be acceptable to large numbers of people in America now. Now they would be described as sexist and ageist.

In the glossary I have already described and explained my forty-five techniques for generating humor. These techniques, I suggest, are the building blocks of all humor and are found, in varying combinations, in all genres of humor. In a joke, we typically find a series of *jokemes* that generate a story or narrative that ends in a punch line, where the expectations established by the narrative are violated in some surprising way.

A Case Study

Let us use the example of the man who goes to Miami—the joke told earlier. I listed nine elements of the narrative when telling the joke:

1. A man goes to Miami for a vacation.
2. After a few days there he looks in a mirror and notices he has a beautiful tan all

over his body, with the exception of his penis.
3. *He decides to remedy the situation so the next morning he goes to a deserted section of the beach, undresses, and covers himself with sand, leaving only his penis exposed to the sun.*
4. *A couple of old ladies walk by.*
5. *One notices the penis sticking out of the sand and points it out to her friend.*
6. *"When I was twenty, I was scared to death of them."*
7. *"When I was forty, I couldn't get enough of them."*
8 *"When I was sixty, I couldn't get one to come near me."*
9. *PUNCH LINE "And now they're growing wild on the beach."*

It is at *Jokeme* 9 that the punch line occurs.

Visually, this joke can be charted as follows:

Jokeme: $1 \rightarrow 2 \rightarrow 3 \rightarrow 4 \rightarrow 5 \rightarrow 6 \rightarrow 7 \rightarrow 8$ Syntagmatic
$$\updownarrow$$
9 Paradigmatic

The joke is linear up until *Jokeme* 8, and then, with *Jokeme* 9, some kind of resolution is established—a resolution that many people find amusing and that often generates laughter. The statement about penises growing wild on the beach establishes a humorous relationship between itself and the first eight statements and is also surprising.

I suggested that it sets up an opposition between nature and culture and that critics with different perspectives on things can interpret the joke in different ways, depending upon their interests and the frame of reference (disciplines, concepts, etc.) they bring to the joke.

What codes are violated? Let me suggest a few. First, the code of privacy. One is not supposed to show one's private parts in public, so we have the opposition: private/public. Second, there is the matter of sexual desire which is supposed to be kept hidden, so we have the opposition: hidden/revealed. And we have the matter of the sexual appetites of elderly women, appetites that we generally tend to assume, in our conventional wisdom, are dormant. This leads to the opposition: dormant/alive. The man who desires the perfect tan violates a code that says trying to be perfect in every way can be defeating. This violation might be described as: perfectionism/good enough-ism or narcissism/self-effacement. Finally, we have the mistake made by the woman who assumes that penises are growing wild on the beach. This mistake leads to the opposition: correct/mistaken.

Humor and a Communication Model

Let me conclude by placing jokes in the wider context of communication theory. This is done in the chart that follows.

Table 2.1: A Communications Model and Humor

A	Communicates B	to C	Via D	Using Form E
Comedian	Information	Audience	TV	Jokes
Writer		Public	Radio	Plays
Cartoonist		Group	Print	Cartoons
Clown		Crowd	Self	Gestures
Actor/ress			Speech	Stories
Sender	Contents	Receiver	Medium	Art Form

and Technique F	With X Effect	For Y Purpose
45 Techniques	Humor	Tension relief
	Laughter	Affiliation
	Mirth	Sexual Arousal
	Joy	Masked Aggression
Technique	Effect	Function

Depending upon our interests, we can focus on individual parts of this model or several at the same time. Using the techniques described in the glossary, it is possible, for example, to study how a humorist evolved, which techniques he or she utilized most, and what this might mean.

Or, if we can get a representative sample of jokes told by a particular group of people—racial, ethnic, socioeconomic, geographical (or some combination of these aspects)— in addition to analyzing the subjects dealt with, we can also see if there are certain techniques that tend to be commonly used. This will give us an added perspective on the social, psychological, and political dimensions of these jokes.

Analyzing a joke means we "kill" it. You can only "cut up" a joke after it's dead just as we only dissect dead bodies in medical school. But we only can analyze the joke after we've heard it and, presumably, enjoyed it or found it interesting. So we are already dealing with a "dead" joke, one might argue. And we can learn a great deal. The patient might die, if it is not already dead, but the operation, we can assume, will always be a success.

PART TWO
APPLICATIONS

3

The Telephone Pole with the Braided Armpits: Ethnic and Racial Jokes and American Society

Ethnic jokes have been around for a long time. Since the first men and women noticed they were different from the second, and ethnocentrism and a sense of ethnic identity appeared, ethnic jokes have been popular. Jokes feed upon differences and distinctions (not only ethnic, of course) and if one of the functions of ethnic jokes is to ridicule and depreciate those in out-groups, another function is to maintain and strengthen a sense of one's identity in some in-group.

Saussure explained in his *Course in General Linguistics* that concepts are "purely differential and defined not by their positive content but negatively by their relations with the other terms of the system" (1966, 117). This notion helps explain how ethnic, religious, and racial groups attain and reinforce their identities—they are the equivalent of "un-colas," they are different in various respects from others, who represent what they are not. Saussure's notion also helps us understand how much ethnic humor works—establishing polar oppositions or paired opposi- tions with the in-group on one side (this is often implicit) and the out-group on the other.

America and the Melting Pot Model

America is a nation of immigrants—each with different customs and traditions and values—and is, par excellence, a breeding ground for ethnic jokes. Among other things, these jokes help release aggressive and hostile feelings in people and, in so doing, help facilitate the relatively peaceful coexistence of different ethnic groups in America. We realize that the notion of America being a huge "melting pot" was an inaccurate metaphor, even though there was a great deal of emphasis on assimilation, on casting off one's ethnic identity and identifying with an American model.

And the model to be imitated was the infamous WASP—the White Anglo-Saxon Protestant. This is not too easy to do when you are Jewish, Catholic, a member of some ethnic minority or a person of color, or some combination of all of these. In recent years, especially since the popularity of "Roots," ethnic, religious, and racial groups have become "in," and now focus on maintaining their identities; the notion of throwing off or escaping from these identities and merging into the great melting pot has been abandoned in large measure. This is reflected even in the highly individuated "ethnic" faces of many of our movie stars, some of whom even speak with easily identifiable accents.

Ethnic Riddles

Let us look at some of the typical ethnic jokes—many of which assume the form of a riddle and are not actually jokes, in that they are not narratives with punch lines. The techniques found in these riddles generally involve ridicule and insult.

Q. Did you hear about the Polish fish?
A. It drowned.

Q. Who was the first telephone Pole?
A. Alexander Graham Kowalski.

Q. How do you break a Pole's finger?
A. Punch him in the nose.

Q. Why does the pope have TGIF embroidered on his bed slippers?
A. To remind him, Toes Go In First.

Q. What has an IQ of 375?
A. Poland

Q. How can you tell the brides at Italian weddings?
A. They're the ones with the braided armpits.

Q. What is the gear makeup in Italian tanks?
A. Four reverses and one forward, in case they are attacked from the rear.

Q. How does a JAP (Jewish American Princess) get exercise?
A. "Waitress!" (waving her arms frantically)

Q. How do you tickle a JAP?
A. Gucci, Gucci, coo!

The fact that these ethnic slurs are riddles tells us something interesting. The riddle is a form of humor based on questions and answers. The questions are about some ethnic group and the answers are some form of insult which leads to a reinforcing of stereotypes and hostile feelings.

It may be that ethnic humor helps us deal with hostility verbally instead of physically, but these slurs also reinforce our stereotypes and sometimes lead to calls for violence. In the case of JAP jokes, for example, they are often done in group settings (at college sport events where people yell "JAP" at women who are dressed in certain ways) and result in public humiliation and shame. We know that when we verbally depreciate the humanity of people it is much easier later to treat them in inhuman ways.

Although riddles are popular with all groups, we start enjoying riddles when we are young and it may be some kind of regression to an earlier state that makes riddling pleasurable. Another reason for our enjoyment may be the element of role reversal; for when we give riddles, we become, for a moment, "superior" to those who are asked to solve the riddles, who are put on the defensive.

Analyzing Ethnic Humor

When we examine ethnic humor, there are four considerations to keep in mind:

- the subject of the humor;
- the form of the humor;
- the techniques in the humor used to generate laughter;
- the themes in the humor.

In the case of much (but not all) ethnic humor, the subject is ethnic groups, such as Italians, Italian Americans, Jews, Poles, Polish Americans, and so on. The form of the humor often is the riddle, though this is not always the case. There are also jokes, comic poems, songs, and parodies, for example. When it comes to techniques we find that insult, ridicule, imitation, use of dialect, revelation of ignorance, mistakes, and stereotyping tend to be dominant.

In the riddles above, Poles are dumb (even the pope), Italians are dirty and cowardly, and Jewish women are materialistic. In England, I found that many of the same jokes that Americans tell about Poles are told about the Irish. Quite likely the same jokes are told in other countries about different minority groups.

Stereotypes are group-shared beliefs that people have about other people and are picked up from families, friends, folklore, and the mass media. The humor reinforces the stereotypes and provides listeners with an understanding of motivation in the humor. The stereotype that Scots are cheap explains, so to speak, why they act the way they do in jokes about them. When we find out that Scots are involved in jokes, we wait for the resolution which involves some manifestation of their cheapness or, in some cases, canniness (or both). There usually is some carryover from the jokes we tell about ethnic groups to our notions about what people are actually like.

In *Ethnic Humor Around the World* (1990), Christie Davies lists various sets of polar oppositions found in ethnic jokes. I have elicited a number of the most important sets of paired opposites from his book.

Stupid	Canny (including sly, shrewd)
Dirty	Clean
Avaricious	Generous (also spendthrifts)
Cowardly	Militaristic (also brave)
Egalitarian	Hierarchical
Common people	The gentry
Boastful	Reserved
Crude	Sophisticated
Lazy	Industrious
Majority	Minority
Central	Peripheral
In-Groups	Out-groups
Static	Dynamic (and enterprising)
Right Foods	Unacceptable foods
Whites	People of color

Davies also lists almost thirty countries where "stupid" and "canny" jokes are told and points out that other countries could be added to the list. The countries include the United States, Canada, Mexico, most of the countries in Western and Eastern Europe, India, Pakistan, China, Russia, and Australia. These two linked oppositions about the stupid and the canny are, he suggests, "the dominant ethnic jokes of the modern world" (1990,12), though other kinds of ethnic jokes are also popular. There are also jokes about snobbish Englishmen, drunken Irishmen, lazy and dirty Mexicans, cowardly Italians, lazy and oversexed blacks, and many others.

There is a question in my mind about whether all the humor that we describe as ethnic actually is ethnic. That is, I'm not sure whether the humor is always aimed at the ethnicity (and distinctive ethnic character- istics) of groups or whether, in many cases, it is aimed at their socioeco- nomic status and marginality. It may be that many of the attacks on groups such as Jews, Italians, and the Irish, for example, may *really* be "safe" attacks on what is perceived to be their lower-class (or upper middle- class, in some cases) life-styles rather than their ethnicity, per se. Are "dirty" Italians ridiculed because they are "dirty" (that is, poor im- migrants, living in slums, etc.) or because they are Italians (members of an ethnic out-group)?

Ethnic humor may represent the opposite of ascribed status; ethnic humor may be seen as *ascribed deflation*. The jokes gain currency in part, I would argue, because people crave humor and the pleasurable release of hostile aggression generated by a sense of superiority. Recall Hobbes' definition of humor involving "sudden glory arising from a sudden conception of some eminency in ourselves by comparison with the infirmity of others." Ethnic humor allows us to take comfort in the way we can "deflate" the status of others, and achieve, relatively speaking "superiority". This leads me to suggest that there is often an element of status anxiety involved in ethnic humor—both in terms of the ethnic jokes we tell about other groups and ourselves.

This helps explain the significance of a character such as Archie Bunker, the hero of "All in the Family." He is a working-class slob, a lovable bigot, who is full of anger and prejudice. He was meant, by his creators, to show the stupidity of these feelings but some research evidence suggests that just the opposite occurred with significant portions of the show's audience. These groups felt that he was telling it "like it is" and that their prejudices were being confirmed.

With "All in the Family" those without prejudice were able to get a double payoff: they could vicariously or unconsciously enjoy or participate in Archie Bunker's hostile insulting behavior, in one respect, while they could also condemn his behavior in another respect. They got twice as much pleasure for their humor investment. "All in the Family" was a weaker version of a British situation comedy, "Till Death Do Us Part." It's hero was even more of a racist and bigot than Archie Bunker.

Ethnic and Racial Groups Telling Jokes about Themselves

In contemporary American society, ethnic humor is no longer permissible in the mass media nor in the public domain; this kind of humor is confined to folklore (which cannot be suppressed or legislated against) and to small groups, that is, the private domain. The only exception is in cases where blacks tell jokes about blacks, Catholics about Catholics, Jews about Jews, and so on. We find comedians such as Richard Pryor joking about blacks and Jewish comedians dealing with Jews. Even in these situations, the situation is always perilous, for comedians always face the risk of being thought of as ashamed of their racial or ethnic identity. Woody Allen, for instance, is thought by some Jews to be a "self-hating Jew," because of the way he portrays Jews in his films.

As Mahadev L. Apte writes, in "Ethnic Humor Versus 'Sense of Humor'":

> It appears that the most crucial element in the dissemination and use of ethnic humor is the perceived ambiguity of the speaker's intentions and motives by those who are its target. There is an increased collective sensitivity on the part of minority ethnic groups to their being made the butt of humor because of their past experiences of social, cultural, and political oppression, and of public ridicule and humiliation. (in Berger, Jan./Feb. 1987, 36)

Apte argues in this article that having a sense of humor is a core value in American culture—one that comes into conflict (in the case of ethnic jokes) with another one of our dominant values, especially since 1950, ethnic and cultural pluralism. This latter phenomenon has relegated ethnic humor to the private domain and impinged upon, one might say, the ability of people, especially government figures, to tell ethnic jokes in public situations. When they do tell ethnic jokes, it usually ends in disaster.

D. J. Bennett has written an essay, "The Psychological Meaning of Anti-Negro Jokes" (1964), which deals, among other things, with jokes that blacks tell about themselves. He suggests they do so because "if suffering seems to be inevitable, better learn to enjoy it" (1964, 56). He offers, as an example, the following joke (which I've modified slightly):

> A Southerner walks into a bar in New York with an alligator on a leash. "You serve Niggers here?" he asks. "We serve Negroes, yes," answers the bartender testily. "Fine," says the Southerner. "I'll have a bourbon. Give my alligator a Negro." (1964,56)

(The punch line Bennett uses is "give my alligator a nigger" but it doesn't work as well as the one I have used.) The preposterous nature of this joke, which involves feeding a human being to an alligator, is a shock. We are unprepared for it, since the joke seems to be about the South and the North (New York) and the matter of racism. The term *serve* is, we find, used in different ways by the southerner and the northern bartender.

Thirty years ago, a babysitter of mine, an Italian-American young woman, told me a number of Italian riddles which, she said, she and other Italian-Americans told about themselves. They were about Italians being dirty and cowardly. I would tend to doubt that contemporary Italian-Americans would tell these jokes. And that is because, I would suggest, they (and other ethnics) are no longer interested in repudiating their ethnic identities. There may also be another element at work. If a group can tell hostile jokes about itself, it disarms others, by showing these jokes aren't bothersome. But there must also be an element of discomfort and resentment at having been put in the position of being the targets (or seeing oneself as being a potential target) of verbal insults and aggression, whether it be from oneself or others.

The Political Dimensions of Elephant Jokes

It has been suggested by Alan Dundes and Roger Abrahams, in a controversial article on elephant jokes, "On Elephantasy and Elephanticide: The Effect of Time and Place" (1969), that there was an outburst of anti-black jokes around the time that the Civil Rights movement was beginning. These elephant jokes, or more precisely riddles, were, on the face of it, about elephants. But the elephants, they suggested, were really (and this functioned on the unconscious level) blacks. There are, the authors point out, many parallels between white stereotypes of blacks (as superstuds) and the way the elephant is portrayed. Many of the jokes dealt with the superhuman sexual prowess of elephants, huge animals from Africa.

Q. How does the elephant find his tail in the dark?
A. Delightful.

Q. How do you know when an elephant's in bed with you?
A. Nine months later you have a problem.

Q. Do you know how to make an elephant fly?
A. Make a zipper about 20 inches long.

Dundes and Abrahams point out how silly and regressive many of the elephant jokes are, but add that a psychoanalytic explanation of the gratifications these jokes offer (which tend to revolve around the Oedipus Complex) is not enough. There are also social and political dimensions to these jokes, which became prominent in the 1960s:

> The development of the black freedom movement, causing anxiety even among those sympathetic to the movement, would seem to be the catalytic agent producing such a regressive response. (Dundes, 1987, 54)

That is, the movement generated a great deal of anxiety among whites who then dealt with these feelings, unconsciously, by telling elephant jokes. Joke cycles, such as elephant jokes or light bulb jokes, Dundes suggests, often are connected to social and political events, and as such, are useful texts for sociologists and political scientists to analyze.

Davies argues in *Ethnic Humor Around the World* that ethnic jokes are a means by which joke-tellers suggest, in an excessive or ludicrous manner, that other ethnic groups have serious deficiencies. But there's more to it than this, for not all values are attacked. Ethnic jokes focus on paired oppositions that "relate to commonly experienced ambiguous and indeed contradictory situations, to dilemmas which seem likely to generate uncertainty and ambivalence" (1990, 307). He points out some of the more important sets of oppositions—stupidity and canniness, cowardliness and militarism, and adds, the inevitably contradictory values and pressures of a complex society mean that the individual has to steer his or her way uncertainly between pairs of competing and contradictory demands knowing that an error in either direction could bring failure or the derision of others. Jokes are the balance in an unbalanced world. Ethnic jokes at the expense of other groups depict them as located at one extreme or the other, with all the failure and discomfort that this brings. (1990, 308)

These jokes, Davies suggests, have a hidden didactic quality to them and help people maintain a steady course between two extremes, both of which are appealing in some respects but ultimately are shown as unacceptable.

I would argue that Davies' conclusion downplays the psychological, social, and political impact of ethnic jokes and suggests that they have essentially a moderating impact on the tellers of these jokes. They may, in the sense that they may provide a release for the hostility that the joke tellers feel toward others and thus, the jokes, moderate their behavior, but at the same time, these jokes strengthen negative stereotypes and are divisive. There are many other kinds of jokes that people can tell that help them deal with anxieties and feelings of ambivalence, but they don't have the same negative consequences. Stigma, whether comedic or not, still hurts.

The Politics of Ethnic and Racial Humor

There is a political dimension, then, to ethnic and racial humor, even if it is not obvious. The fact that this humor is no longer acceptable suggests that ethnic and racial minorities have gained enough political power to make it just about impossible to direct hostile humor against ethnic and racial groups (and other groups, such as the disabled) in the media and in public forums. Humor, of course, is an ineluctable force and we cannot prevent ethnic jokes nor riddles from being told (or even published in joke collections). But we have been able to curtail, somewhat, the use of ethnic and racial stereotyping and jokes about ethnic and other groups in the media, and that is a sign of considerable progress.

4

"On Me You Can't Count":
An Interpretation of a Jewish Joke with
Relevance to the Jewish Question

On Me You Can't Count

A little old Jewish man goes up to the receptionist in a very swank, ultramodern corporation. "May I see the director of Human Resources," he says, with a thick Jewish accent. "In what regard?" asks the secretary. "The position advertised in The New York Times," he replies. He is ushered into the office of the director, a young executive, who looks at the old Jewish man in astonishment. "Did you advertise," he asks, with a thick Jewish accent, "for a director of research with a knowledge of multivariate analysis and advanced statistical methods?" "Why yes," answers the executive, wondering whether this old Jewish man might have these abilities. "And did you want someone with at least ten years of experience in a large, multinational organization?" "And you wanted, in addition, someone with an MBA from a top business school?" "Yes," replies the executive. "Well, I just wanted to tell you," says the old man, "on me you can't count."

Oppositions in the Joke

What are we to make of this joke? What's funny about it (if anything)? How does it generate its humor? And what does it have to tell us about the Jews and Jewish humor?

The first thing we notice is that the joke is based upon a set of polar oppositions, which are listed below:

Old	Young
Jew	Gentile
Heavy Accent	Regular Speech
Ethnic	American
Outsider	Insider
Individual	Member of an Organization
Word Order Reversal	Normal Word Order

We find, then, a series of polar oppositions that help define each of the two characters involved in the story. These oppositions suggest that the old Jew is different in many ways from the young executive who interviews him (or is interviewed by him, to be more precise). The old Jew is an individual, but he may also be seen as a symbol of Jewishness—or, at least, of a certain kind of Jewishness. That is, he may be seen as a stereotype of the Jews by non-Jews and as a representative of first generation, Old-World Jews by Jews.

The Significance of the Punch Line

The punch line of this story works in two ways. First, there is the matter of defeated expectations. As we hear the recital of the requirements for the position and carry a picture of the old Jew in our mind's eye, we wonder how the old Jew will fit into the picture. Could he be a legitimate candidate for the position? It seems preposterous, but one never can tell about Jews. Then, we get the punch line, "On me you can't count," which confirms our suspicions that the Jew couldn't fit the specifications of the job.

The second way the punch line works is by its incongruity. The old Jew is clearly from a different world and the contrast between him and all that he represents and the position he is inquiring about is enormous. The question is—what is he doing there at all? He has insinuated himself into a situation where he clearly does not belong.

Absurdity in the Joke

There is also the word order to be considered. When the old Jew says, "On me you . . . " we almost expect him to be applying for the job. It is only the last part of the word can, the negation "can't count," that tells us he's not applying for the job. The situation is absurd then, for we have a man who isn't applying for a job in a place where we would expect someone who is applying for a job to be. What is the old Jew doing there, inquiring about the position, since he doesn't want it?

The Old Jew and the Jewish Question

We have an element of assertiveness, on the part of the old Jew, which strikes us as very odd. He is there because he feels, somehow, that he has to make his position known. It might be looked upon as an extremely egocentric position; in all situations he must make his existence taken into consideration. If we see him as symbolic of the Jews in general, we can say that he represents the assertiveness of the Jews and the feeling that, *ultimately, all things relate to the Jewish Question and the survival of the Jews.*

There are many jokes about the passionate concern Jews have with Jewish survival and the way they focus anything and everything on that matter. A classic joke based on this stereotype follows:

> *The United Nations asks a number of different nationalities and ethnic groups to write books about elephants. They get the following books. The French write a book titled "The Love Life of Elephants." The English write a book "The Elephant and English Social Classes." The Germans write a five volume work titled "A Short Introduction to the History of the Elephant." The Jews write a book, "Elephants and The Jewish Question."*

This joke suggests that Jews are obsessed by the Jewish Question and see everything in terms of that obsession, which involves, ultimately, the survival of the Jews and Judaism.

On Jewish Marginality

It is important to realize that throughout most of their history, the Jews have been a marginal people in most societies and, often, a "despised race." In America, for example, where the "on me you can count" joke takes place, Jews make up approximately 3 percent of the population. That is, 97 percent of the people in America are non-Jews. Considering the high visibility of Jews in America (and in world history), it is hard to believe that there are so few of them.

This marginality is central to understanding Jewish culture and Jewish humor. Judaism is, amongst other things, a highly moralistic religion and Jews have championed civil rights and related causes both out of moral fervor and because they benefit from living in a society of laws. Jews are people of the book and, in America, this has been translated into an extraordinarily high level of educational attainment. Jews have become professional people because in many cases they could not find work in certain areas (barred to them due to anti-Semitism).

Recent statistics suggest that Jews tend to be affluent but by no means wealthy, though, of course, there are some extremely wealthy Jews. They tend to be middle and upper-middle class, and often work in areas that originally had little status and where they found opportunities.

The old Jew in this joke is, obviously, a marginal figure but he is an assertive one who says, in effect, "you've got to take me into account." As marginal people, the Jews have had to use whatever techniques they could to protect their rights, to criticize, to focus attention on social problems, and so on. One of these techniques is humor—which can be used, without threat of retaliation, to focus people's attention on issues of importance.

Humor, Freud suggested, is a form of masked aggression but we can translate this aggression concept, without great difficulty, into something broader, namely social criticism. (It is no accident that the blacks in America have also generated a significant number of humorists. They too have suffered from racism and persecution and they too have come to recognize the power of humor.) There may also be an element of aggression, per se, in much of this humor—which can be used by those with no other means of dealing with their hostility and anger.

On Old-World and New-World Jewish Humor

The old Jewish gentleman of our story is a figure out of the old world. He is, we must assume, a refugee who has not lost his accent. As such, he is a representative of what I would call Old- World Jewish Humor, the humor of the shtetl, which might be contrasted with American New-World Jewish humor, the humor of the suburbs. These two forms of Jewish humor are differentiated in the chart below:

Old-World Jewish Humor	New-World Jewish Humor
Shtetl	Suburb
Poverty	Affluence, Materialism
Warmth	Coldness
Acceptance	Alienation
Rabbis	Professional types, JAPS
Survival	Acceptance

There is a kind of warmth and loving quality to much of the Old-World Jewish humor. It was the humor of a truly oppressed people who, despite their poverty and problems, made room, somehow, for all the bizarre types (schnorrers, schlamatzls, schlemeiels, etc.) who populated their world. There was an open-ness and warmth and good-naturedness re-flected in the jokes and the stories about the people in the shtetls that was remarkable, considering the difficult situation in which the Old-World Jews found themselves.

The New-World Jewish Humor doesn't seem to have this quality. Some of the jokes, especially those about Jewish American Mothers and Jewish American Princesses, reflect a bitterness and perhaps even a kind of self-hatred that seems to afflict many American Jews. For many years the White Anglo-Saxon Protestant was looked upon as the ego-ideal for all Americans and it is only in recent years that this has changed and ethnicity has become respectable or accepted. (Many American Jews, in attempting to distance themselves from the Old-World Jewish identity, have abandoned Judaism, except for a vague cultural identification, if even that).

Jewish American Mothers and Jewish American Princesses

The Jewish American Princess stories make fun of young Jewish American women for being materialistic, being overly concerned with clothes and fashion, and for wanting to avoid sex and cooking.

How does a Jewish Princess commit suicide?
She piles all of her clothes on top of a bed and jumps off.

What's the ideal house for a Jewish Princess?
6000 square feet with no bedroom and no kitchen.

What does a Jewish American Princess make for dinner?
Reservations.

The Jewish American Princess is, obviously, a polar opposite of the Jewish American Mother. These oppositions are reflected in the chart below:

Jewish American Mother	Jewish-American Princess
Has children	Avoids sex
Sacrifices for children	Self-centered existence
Cooks	Won't cook
Housewife role basic	Avoids housewife functions
Overly concerned about kids	Overly concerned about self
Scrimps and Saves	Spends money
Jewishness basic	Americaness basic

The Jewish American Princess is created by the Jewish American Mother who is then repudiated by her creation. The Jewish American Princess has turned her back on Old-World Jewishness and has become hyper-American. She has picked up the worst of American culture, its gross materialism and self-centeredness. She also, it seems, has illusions about her status—seeing herself, somehow, as a "princess." If, somehow, she does have children, they will become JAPITS—Jewish American Princesses (or Princes) In Training.

These Jewish American Princess jokes reflect, I would suggest, the hostility that many Jewish American males feel about their mothers, which is then transferred onto their wives. It may also be connected with the anxiety many Jewish American males feel about their relationships with their wives—which is based on their role as good providers more than feelings of love and affection. Also, there may be elements of anger about the way some Jewish women act, recognizing that they are in great demand (or were, at least, before intermarriage became so widespread). Mostly, I would suggest, they reflect a kind of self-hatred many Jewish American males feel about their Jewishness and their marginality in American society.

It is a damaging stereotype that poisons relationships among Jewish males and females and that has been picked up by non-Jews and used by some of them to justify their anti-Jewish beliefs.

On Me You Can't Count

The old Jewish man, who "interviews" for the job, obviously is from a different world, and is a person who does not know how to behave, how to get along in American society. He has not learned to speak like other Americans and thus, horror of horrors, is immediately identifiable as a Jew. This, curiously, does not seem to bother him at all. And he certainly does not know his place in the world.

The old Jewish man of the joke accepts his Jewishness and, more than that, asserts it in the face of a society that is, at best, not concerned and, at worst, hostile. When the old Jewish man tells the director of human resources, "On me you can't count," he is asserting his importance, as a Jew, and, ultimately, the importance of all Jews. "You've got to take people like me into consideration," he is saying, "and in this particular situation, I want you to know that I can't be of any help to you." That information, he obviously feels, is of importance. It is an assertion of his (and by implication of his people's) dignity in a world in which Jews, humane values, and many other things seem in danger of becoming irrelevant.

Conclusions

There are a number of things that are humorous about this joke. First, there is the use of dialect humor. We may find dialects humorous because they make those of us who speak without a dialect feel superior. Whatever the case, dialect is an important humorous device, especially when the dialect is congruous with the values, beliefs and behavior of the ethnic or regional group that is the subject of the joke.

Then there is the matter of defeated expectations. There are elements of the shaggy dog story in this joke (especially if the section on the qualifications of the person desired are expanded upon, which can easily be done). After the long repetition of the qualifications, the would-be interviewee turns the tables and tells the interviewer that he isn't interested in the position.

In addition, there is the element of incongruity. I listed the oppositions in this text, which reveal the polarities involved in the story and give us some insights into why the old Jew has come to the fancy organization.

What are we to make of a person who goes to an organization and informs the person in charge of human resources that he is *not* applying for a position for which he is obviously unsuited? What we see may be an example of an incredible sense of chutzpah, in which the old Jew feels that he is at the center of the universe and everything revolves around him.

More likely, as I have suggested, it is an existential statement and one that has interesting sociological implications. If we see the corporation as a metaphor for modern society and a position in it as a means of belonging to modern society, or fitting in (and, in the process, abandoning one's heritage and Judaism), the old Jew is making a strong statement about his identity and sense of self-worth.

"On me you can't count," then, becomes not so much a statement as a challenge—to the forces of modernity and attendant forces of assimilation (tied, in part, to shame and Jewish self-hatred). "On me you can't count," the old Jew says to the Human Resources Director, but at the same time, he is saying to God, "On me you can count!"

5

Jewish Fools:
From the Wise Men of Chelm to Jackie Mason

There are a number of problems involved in writing about Jewish fools. It's difficult to say what a Jew is. Are Jews a people with a particular religion, a people who answer questions with questions, a race, or something else? (I used the term *race* so I could mention Louis Untermeyer's wonderful quip about Jews, plastic surgeons, and "nose jobs"—that Jews are people who cut off their noses to spite their race.)

The Jewish response to a question about what Jews are, or how to categorize Jews would be "Why do you want to know?" I will assume that people who are raised as Jews and think they are Jewish and whom other people think are Jewish are Jewish—though, as some recent news stories about "lost" or "hidden" Jews reveal, a number of of people who weren't raised as Jews and thought they weren't Jewish are discovering, to their great surprise, that they are Jewish.

Jewish Fools

How are Jewish fools different from all other fools? And how is Jewish humor different from all other humor? We will take Avner Ziv's suggestion that "Jewish humor is the humor created by Jews, reflecting special aspects of Jewish life" (*Humor* 1991, 4–2:145) as our starting point. This humor has, he adds, an intellectual, a social, and an emotional dimension to it—though he points out that his definition tends to be psychological and that there are other perspectives on Jewish humor to be considered.

Jewish fools, by being Jewish and thus experiencing, to varying degrees, marginality, powerlessness, and persecution (among other things), are different from non-Jewish fools and from other Jewish comic characters, though the difference between fools, per se, and other Jewish droll characters (especially those from the East European shtetls) is sometimes hard to explain. In the shtetls we found a number of comic types such as the luftmensch (the man who lives on air, who is also sometimes a luckless dreamer) and the shlimazl (the man who has bad luck, the eternal loser). When a shlemiel spills soup, as he invariably does, he spills it on a shlimazl). A shlemiel, according to Leo Rosten in *The Joys of Yiddish* is a foolish person, a simpleton, a consistently unlucky person, a clumsy all-thumbs gauche type, a social misfit, a pipsqueak, a naive, trusting gullible customer, or someone who makes foolish bargains or bets (1971, 352–53). Rosten, in this characterization, provides us with a list of attributes of fools that shows there are many different kinds.

The first fools, Harry Levin suggests in *Playboys and Killjoys*, were "harmless halfwits" who were taken in as "mascots" in large feudal households (1987, 51). They evolved in two directions: one was the natural fool, the "domestic imbecile" whose antics people found entertaining and the other was the artificial fool, a professional entertainer who played the role of the fool, who was witty and made telling comments while pretending he was a simpleton. Among the real fools, as the fool figure was taken up in society, there are also gradations: some are imbeciles, but others are types of people who for one reason or another are looked upon as foolish.

Jews call certain kinds of fools "putzes" (a *putz*, Rosten says, is a slang term for penis, as is the Yiddish term *schmuck*)—though this is a somewhat contemptuous term for: "1. a fool, an ass, a jerk and 2. a simpleton, a yokel; an easy mark" (1971,306). This discussion of Jewish comic types suggests that there are a number of different kinds of Jewish fools or aspects to Jewish foolishness, which need to be differentiated from one another. There are, I would suggest, two basic fool figures: the natural Jewish fool (of whom there are many subcategories, to be discussed below) and the jester figure, the Jewish entertainer who plays the fool, who takes on the role of the fool, for one or another reasons.

A Typology of Natural Jewish Fools

What follows is a typology of Jewish fools, a list of the different kinds of fools one might find in folktales about the shtetl and in contemporary comic routines—not that they are mutually exclusive, mind you. Some characters are foolish in a number of different ways at the same time. (I am focusing on male fools here but everything I say can be applied, in principle, to women, as well, though in Jewish humor Jewish women tend to be portrayed as spoiled bitches or self-sacrificing types.)

1. *Fools have poor judgment.* They can be persuaded to do things that are not in their self-interest, they make bets that can't be won, they consider marrying, and often marry, women who are highly undesirable on the basis of their physical attributes, personalities, or both.

   A schadken brings a customer to the house of a potential bride. The man is amazed. "She's beautiful," says the man. "She has lovely blonde hair, a wonderful figure and is very pretty." "Yes," says the schadken. "I thought you'd like her. There is one thing—she's slightly pregnant."

2. *Fools are innocent, naive.* They lack information about the world and how to function in it. They are not cynical, skeptical, and paranoid like "normal" people. Gimpel, the fool, the hero of Singer's celebrated story, is an example of this kind of figure.

3. *Fools use crazy logic.* They do not reason well and on the basis of their absurd logic often end up coming to absurd conclusions or doing ridiculous things. The "wise men" of Chelm are this kind of fool.

4. *Fools have crazy ideas.* They are harmlessly deranged but usually are tolerated by people who have compassionate feelings toward them (thinking, perhaps, "there, but for God, go I").

5. *Fools are monomaniacs.* Fools have some fixation that motivates them, some passion, some mad notion, that shapes or dominates every aspect of their lives. Jack Benny's fixation on saving money, his cheapness, is an example of this kind of fool. Benny happened on to this identity by accident. Mail, after one of his shows, was very favorable about a bit on Benny being cheap. Eventually, Benny developed a comic identity based on cheapness. A classic example is the famous scene in which a robber comes up to Benny, points a gun at him, and says "Your money or your life." After a long silence Benny says "I'm thinking it over."

6. *Fools are stupid.* They lack information, they lack knowledge, they are childish, they do stupid things. In Yiddish these characters are often called schmucks (literally penises but also dopes, jerks, boobs).

7. *Fools are nuisances.* They get in the way, they prevent people from doing things they want to do, and they are hard to get rid of.

8. *Fools are social misfits and jerks*. They lack an understanding of how to function in society and don't recognize what people think of them. Some subcategories of the jerk, or figures who are close to the jerk are pompous asses, dandies and fops, and boasters (alazons).

9. *Fools are unlucky*. Everything they try turns out wrong and they are often made foolish by others (as in the case of the shlimazl, who is always having soup spilled on him by shlemiels). Nebechs, poor souls, unlucky types, are also in this category. As Rosten points out, when a shlemiel spills soup on a shlimatzl, the nebech cleans up.

(Orrin E. Klapp has written an interesting book, *Heroes, Villains and Fools: The Changing American Character* [1962], which deals with the roles these figures play in American culture and society and he has an elaborate typology of different kinds of American fools that readers may find worth consulting.)

This list suggests that there can be many different kinds of fools, and what a fool is like is a consequence of whether he has one or more of the above characteristics. We also can see from this list that sometimes (perhaps more often than we imagine) wise men act foolishly just as, sometimes, fools might act in a wise manner. If we think of the wise man being at one end of a continuum and the fool at the other end, most of us fall somewhere in between these two extremes, with some of us closer to one or the other polarity.

The Functions of Jewish Fools

Saussure (1966) explained that concepts gained meaning by differentiation; the Jewish fool, especially when we talk about the shtetl, has to be seen as the opposite of the figure of the Talmudic scholar, the "wise man," who was the ideal of the people in the shtetl. As Irving Howe and Eliezer Greenberg point out in the introduction they wrote to *A Treasury of Yiddish Stories*, "Scholarship . . . was extraordinarily honored among the Jews. One's prestige, authority, and position depended to a considerable extent on one's learning" (1974,4).

If the ego ideal of the Eastern European Jews was the scholar, and in particular the Talmudic scholar, his opposite, and the figure that best gave him definition was the fool, the ignoramus, the dunce. We can understand the illogicality of the mythical "wise men" of Chelm, a town of fools, in the context of a society that honored scholars, sages, and those capable of achieving the most remarkable feats of logic and interpretation of the Torah.

The fool also provides a bit of relief from being reasonable, a release from the burden of wisdom and logic, a momentary regression to a state somewhat like childhood when we were not held responsible for our actions and were not expected to be logical. The chart below shows these oppositions in graphic form.

Talmudic Scholar	Fool
high status	low status
logical	absurd
wisdom	stupidity
tension	ease

This polar opposition is still meaningful, though we have replaced the figure of the Talmudic scholar with a secularized version—the professional person (professor, doctor, lawyer, accountant, MBA)—and we have replaced the fool with the comedian.

The comedian, the funnyman, the actor who plays humorous roles— all of these people can be seen as fools, but there is a difference: these people are *eirons*, people pretending to be fools, people who play the role of the fool. And like the fools of earlier times, these fools have an ironic fate: the wisdom these fools speak (when they speak wisdom, that is) is generally not taken seriously. This is because, of course, they are fools and to be a fool means nobody takes you seriously (or is supposed to take you seriously).

Perspectives on Jewish Fools and Jewish Humor

Fools, ancient and modern, can be interpreted from a number of perspectives. We have already discussed the way fools in the shtetls set off and help define Talmudic scholars. The existence of these fools also can be seen as a criticism of the sometimes arid scholarship that was found in the Talmudic academies of Eastern Europe. In a more general way, fools offer figures for ordinary people to feel superior to, which, as Aristotle pointed out, is an important element in humor. Nobody is lower than fools in the scale of things.

In addition, playing the fool (or having professional fools who speak for them) allows Jews to mask the aggression that many of them feel but find difficult to express due to their marginality and, historically, their powerlessness and anxiety. There is also the matter, already dealt with, of regressing and escaping the burden of being logical and rational and, in extreme cases, of being a scholar and thus being judged by one's intellect. As Ziv points out, in the introduction to the issue of *Humor* that he edited, being able to laugh at life or reality tends to make it more tolerable and less frightening (1991, 4-2:146).

From a sociological perspective, Jewish fools keep Jews alert and also focus attention on social justice and other matters of a similar nature that impact on Jewish life. Jewish humor has a social dimension to it, and also often reflects the moralism and stress on justice that are so much part of Jewish thought and culture.

Now I will examine a sampling of Jewish fools, starting with the "wise men" of Chelm.

The Fools of Chelm

Chelm is a town in Poland that became famous in folklore as a town full of fools. As Nathan Ausubel writes in *A Treasury of Jewish Folklore*,

> What is Chelm? It is a real town in Poland, like Gotham in England and and Schildburg in Germany. These three towns have one thing in common—for some unaccountable reason they were elected in irreverent folklore to serve as centers of innocent stupidity. (1978, 320)

Ausubel points out that tales of Schildburg's fools were translated into Yiddish in 1597 and were very popular. He suggests that there were many stories about fools in Yiddish at the time and that Chelm may have provided people with a peg on which they could hang all their stories about fools. He adds, about the Chelm stories:

> They not only have Jewish settings and, to some extent, are an index to Jewish character, customs and manners, but they also possess many facets of Jewish irony and wit. (1948,321)

That is why the stories are frequently described as being about the "wise men" of Chelm or reflecting the "wisdom" of Chelm. Generally speaking, the fools of Chelm think and act in illogical and ridiculous ways. Here is one story from Chelm:

A young scholar from Chelm was shocked when after only three months of marriage his wife gave birth to a child. He went running to the rabbi. "Rabbi," he said, "Although we've only been married for three months, my wife has just given birth to a child. How can this be?" "I can see," said the rabbi, "that you don't know about such things. Let me ask a few questions. You said you have lived with your wife for three months, is that not so." "Yes," said the scholar. "And she has lived with you for three months, is that not so?" "Yes," said the scholar. "And you have lived together for three months, also . . . is that not so?" "Yes," said the scholar. "If you add them all up, what do you get?" "Nine months," said the scholar.

Here is another very famous Chelm tale:

An inhabitant of Chelm loses his keys and enlists his friends to help him find them. They search around near a light in the village. "Is this where you lost your keys?" asks a friend. "No," says the man, "but the light is better here."

In both of these stories the inhabitants of Chelm display a lack of intelligence, though there is a semblance of logic to their behavior. In the first story, the rabbi gets the count up to nine months by playing loose with logic and in the second story, the searchers look for the key where they have light (which is reasonable, but only if the key was dropped in that area). If they weren't fools they would have brought light to the area where the key was dropped.

The stories about the fools of Chelm served as a counter to the reverent stories about Talmudic scholars, who used reason and logic so remarkably and brilliantly in their *pilpul* exercises (perhaps splitting hairs at times), and also may have intimated that these scholars, in pursuing their study of the Torah so single-mindedly, were in certain ways foolish. In recent years, Poland itself, for some reason, was turned by jokelore into a country of fools who acted in stupid ways (the same process of foolification has been done to other countries as well, as Christie Davies has shown in his work on ethnic humor). And one joke about the number of Poles it takes to change a light bulb led to a series of light bulb jokes in America that ridiculed different ethnic and social groups—Mexicans, Jewish mothers, Californians, graduate students, WASPish society women, and so on.

Zusia, the "Fool of God"

Zusia and his brother Elimelekh were two brothers who Elie Wiesel tells us were "the great figures of Galician Hasidism toward the end of the eighteenth century" (1973, 114). In *Souls on Fire* Wiesel recounts the story of these men, both of whom were *tzaddiks* (rabbis, leaders, holy men). Zusia, was a "fool of God" and his brother was a serious thinker and the founder of a major school of Hassidic thought.

Wiesel recounts a story that is of interest. The brothers, while still leading an anonymous life, were in an inn where a wedding was being celebrated. When some of the guests got drunk they decided to have some fun with the two guests who were huddled in the back of the hearth. Wiesel writes,

> For no particular reason, Zusia was the one they grabbed. They made him twirl and stumble and let the blows rain on him before letting him go. An hour later they started all over. And so it went until late into the night. (1973,114)

When his brother Elimelekh sought to switch places, the drunkards, not recognizing who they had, cried out that they had beaten the first person (Zusia) enough and should beat the other one, so they let Elimelekh go and grabbed Zusia again. Zusia's explanation was "You see? It's not up to us; we are powerless. Everything is written" (1973,114).

Zusia, through no fault of his own, was forced into the role of the fool, of "he who gets slapped." And he continued in that role during his life. His brother, on the other hand, became a powerful and important tzaddik. The brothers, Wiesel suggests, both contributed to the way rabbis were formed. As Wiesel puts it,

> Without either, Hasidism would have been different. Together they gave its future a countenance. In years to come, for a Rebbe to be whole, he had to be both Rebbe Zusia—innocence and humility personified—and Rebbe Elimelekh, supreme incarnation of authority and power. Their two portraits—so distinct and yet intertwined— have remained singularly alive in Hasidic memory. (1973,115)

The Hasidic movement, which is still alive and flourishing, has generated rabbis who combine these elements; this combination, I would suggest, is also found in the personalities of many Jewish people. (As we will see in my analysis of Jackie Mason, it is possible to have a rabbi and a fool or jester figure/comedian in one person.)

Gimpel, the Fool

Let's consider how Singer's story begins:

I am Gimpel the fool. I don't think of myself as a fool. On the contrary. But that's what folks call me.

In the first few sentences of this story we see the power of labeling. Gimpel has been assigned a role in his town—that of a fool. When he says, "I am Gimpel the fool," he is not describing the way he sees himself. As he points out, "I don't think of myself as a fool. On the contrary."

This beginning poses an interesting problem: do fools always realize they are fools? Is it possible that large numbers of people who don't think of themselves as fools, who may (on the contrary) think of themselves as wise, actually are fools. And is it possible that many people who think of themselves as fools and who may be perceived by others as fools, are actually intelligent or even wise?

Why doesn't Gimpel say "I am Gimpel"? Because that wouldn't tell us very much about him. No, he has to say something about who or what he is, other than his name, so we will be able to understand the significance of what happens to him.

Gimpel's problem is that he is gullible, that he believes people. He doesn't learn to be cynical about human motives and skeptical about human goodness the way normal people do. "I believed everyone," he tells us, adding a bit later, "In the first place, everything is possible." Gimpel is a fool because he believes in human goodness. As a result of his gullibility he is given an identity, by his townsfolk, of a fool. "The whole town came down on me," he tells us, "so I had to believe."

They play numerous jokes on him. They tell him all kinds of ridiculous things and he seems to believe them. Actually, he tells us he doesn't, but rather he more or less plays along with the townsfolk. We see here the power that humor, and, in particular, group laughter, has to coerce and control people, to affect their values, beliefs, and even their identities.

The logic is inescapable. Since everyone defines Gimpel as a fool, and treats him as one, he must accept that social identity. He helps everyone, of course, by believing (or seeming to believe) all the crazy things people tell him. This is understandable to one who is a possibilitarian, who thinks that "everything is possible," and not to those who believe nothing is possible. There is also, I should point out, a feeling of care, maybe even of love for Gimpel, found in the townspeople. They have a fool on their hands, but he is also a wonderful baker, and they want to make sure he stays around for a good long time.

Thus, Gimpel is pushed into a marriage with a whore, who won't sleep with him on his wedding night (and seldom thereafter, one infers) but who bears many children from liasons with other men. But Gimpel, being a fool, does not seem to realize that the children are not his. He loves the children and takes joy in them. He often finds his wife sleeping with another man, but in each case he is told that he is seeing things or has misunderstood what is going on.

For Gimpel, the world we know, the world our senses bring to us, is not the real world. What is real is the world to come. As he tells us:

> No doubt the world is entirely an imaginary world, but it is only once removed from the true world.

Given this, the tricks that the townspeople play on him are relatively trivial from his perspective.

In certain respects, some elements of this story reminds one of a number of jokes—some Jewish and some non-Jewish. Gimpel's marriage to the whore calls to mind all the jokes about schadken in the shtetls. They are always trying to marry off women who are old, cross-eyed, walk with limps, are hard of hearing, or, occasionally, even "slightly" pregnant (as was Gimpel's wife). In other respects, the story reminds one of all the jokes that deal with how men with savoir-faire react when they find their wives in bed with another man. In a curious way, we might argue, Gimpel has savoir-faire.

When his wife is dying, she confesses that none of the children are his, but Gimpel is not destroyed. And after her death Gimpel dreams of her at night and sees her in a glorified manner. At this point, he is well off, so he divides the money up among the children and sets off on a voyage of self-discovery. When he still lived in the town and worked as a baker, he had been tempted by the devil and urinated in a batch of dough—though he buried the bread after it was baked (and we can't be sure this episode wasn't a bad dream). He sees his dead wife, Elka, wearing a shroud in a dream and she cautions him:

> Because I was false is everything false too? I never deceived anyone but myself. I'm paying for it all, Gimpel. They spare you nothing here.

Only the rabbi in his shtetl sees things as they really are. The rabbi tells Gimpel that he isn't a fool but that the townspeople are all fools, despite their knowledge. And the rabbi says that they will pay dearly for their behavior. This is because, under Jewish law, causing a person to feel shame leads to a loss of paradise. That is, it prevents one from entering the paradise of the world to come, a paradise that those who are kind and innocent will surely inhabit.

The tale can also be seen as something of an allegory. In this light, Gimpel represents the Jewish people—those who believe in the Torah and are kind to others and humble before God. It is the Jews, who believe "everything is possible." Around them is a hostile majority of people with different beliefs and practices. They define the Jews as fools—people who haven't accepted the new revelations, who are unable to see the truth.

As fools or outcasts, as a "despised people" (as the Jews have been called), as unbelievers, anything that Christians or any others do to them is seen as acceptable. Gimpel's wife is a representative figure, who mistreats Gimpel all the time, and lies to him continually. Gimpel, as the paradigmatic Jew, endures all of this until he can escape from his torments, which he does when his wife dies and he is not bound by a "foolish" sense of responsibility toward her or her children. He then becomes a wandering Jew, searching for wisdom and peace in foreign lands, where the stigma from his previous identity no longer can torment him. In the paradise that awaits him, Gimpel knows, he will find happiness. "Whatever may be there," he says, "it will be real, without complication, without ridicule, without deception. God be praised: there even Gimpel cannot be deceived."

Singer's story is rich in symbolism and full of ambiguities. For modern and postmodern people, who do not believe in the devil, let alone God and the world to come, this tale of the shtetl and Gimpel's naiveté, his acceptance of twenty years of abuse by his wife and the townspeople, must seem very strange. We are taught not to "suffer fools gladly," but "Gimpel the Fool" raises an interesting question—who are the real fools? Singer doesn't answer this question, but he plants a worm of doubt that might give many of us something to think about.

Jackie Mason: The Rabbi and Fool Merge

There are any number of Jewish comedy writers, comedians, comic actors, and so on who deserve attention: Jack Benny, the Marx Brothers, Don Rickles, Woody Allen, Sid Caesar, George Burns, Jerry Lewis—the list goes on and on. And as Ziv pointed out in his introduction to the special edition of *Humor* (1991) on Jewish humor, at one time, a few decades ago, something like 80 percent of the most successful humorists were Jewish. Since Jews make up about 3 percent of the population, they were overrepresented by a factor of more than twenty-five to one in this area.

I hope that my discussion of Jewish fools has suggested some of the reasons why Jews have become comedians. In part, it may have been because they couldn't get into other professions very easily. But it also probably has something to do with the Jewish fool figure as it has evolved over the years. And now, with Jackie Mason, a rabbi who makes his living as a stand-up comedian and plays on his Jewishness very strongly, we have the combination of fool and authority figure that Wiesel mentioned in his discussion of Zusia and his brother Elimelekh.

Many of the Jewish comedians before Mason kept their Jewishness discreetly hidden and may have been quite ambivalent about it themselves. Mason, on the other hand, uses Jewishness and the difference between Jews and gentiles as one of his major subjects. He presents himself as a personification of what might be called the "Jewish observer" and uses his stance to create humor. Like many stand-up comedians, he doesn't tell jokes very often but offers, instead, amusing and often highly perceptive insights into the contemporary scene. He comes off as part anthropologist, part sociologist, part comedian/fool.

In his show "The World According to Me" his basic subject is the difference between Jews and other people; sometimes gentiles, per se, but other times ethnic groups such as Italians, Puerto Ricans, or Poles. His stance is that of a Jew who is explaining, in the best tradition of the rabbi (which means "teacher"), some of the curious customs and folkways of the Jews in America and of other ethnic groups. He has a lot to say about Jewish husbands, Jewish wives, Jews in Beverly Hills, Jews going on vacation, Jewish occupations, Jewish sex—and he uses a good deal of Yiddish in his performance.

Among his basic techniques are stereotyping, exaggeration, and insults (that are not meant to be taken seriously, of course). There are no cockroaches, he says, in white Anglo-Saxon Protestant houses because there's no food in them (only liquor). But in Jewish homes, he adds, the cockroaches are enormous as the result of all the food that's around—cheese danishes, for example. The stereotype he plays on is that gentiles drink and Jews eat. He compares pieces of cake sold in Jewish restaurants to those sold in gentile restaurants. The gentiles get tiny little slices of cake, what Jews think of as cookies. But in Jewish restaurants, the portions are huge and when they are served, the patrons complain that the size of the portions is going down.

One of his themes is the attempts Jews make to fit in, and to show how successful they are. This, he explains, is why Jews buy boats. "There's no bigger schmuck in the world than a Jew with a boat." Jews, he adds, know nothing about boating and don't even know when some gentile salesman sells them a boat without a motor. All Jews know or care about is how many the boat sleeps. "This boat sleeps six," they say or "my boat sleeps twelve." Having a boat, he asserts, is something that gentiles do, not Jews.

From time to time he talks about politics, and has something to say about Ronald Reagan—who he portrays as a kind of nitwit—and Richard Nixon. "I always liked Richard Nixon," Mason says. "I like a crook who knows his job." After a discussion of presidents, Congress, and deficits, he concludes that what America needs is a Jewish president, so the country can show a profit. It's not a job for a gentile, he explains.

He also complains about the Chinese. Jews, he points out, spend their lives (so it seems) eating in Chinese restaurants, but the Chinese, he says, never eat in Jewish restaurants. He's never had a Chinaman ask where he could get a nice piece of gefilte fish. Mason also uses the technique of reversal in discussing tough Jews. You never see tough Jews, he tells us. Can you ever imagine four blacks seeing a Jew saying, "Watch out, there's a Jew?"

A Jewish man may have a position of prominence in some organization. He's a partner (a word Jews love, Mason suggests), people may bow and scrape to him—but when he gets home his wife says "You schmuck!" Jewish wives don't cook, always want to go on vacation, take incredible amounts of clothing with them, and, generally, dominate their husbands. He compares the situation with Italians. Italian wives live in terror, are always cooking sauces in the kitchen (even at 4:00 A.M. in the event their husband comes home and is hungry), and are very subservient. Italian women are always asking, "Did I do something wrong, Tony?" When an Italian man goes off to work, his wife asks, "Are you coming back, Tony?" Not so with a Jewish wife.

You have to see Jackie Mason in person, or listen to his record, to get a sense of his style. There's a cadence to his performance, a rhythm that he maintains that is very important as well as the way he inflects his voice, uses Yiddish phrases, pokes fun at people in the audience, and creates the persona of an offbeat commentator on life, and in particular, on things Jewish and non-Jewish. With Mason, the jester part of the fool/jester combination has become dominant. He can say the many insulting things he does about Jews, gentiles, Italians, Poles, Puerto Ricans, politicians—you name it—because of his comic persona, which tells us we are not to take him seriously. The jester establishes a play frame within which he works to achieve his goals—laughter and what often comes with it, insight. Instead of offering a *drosh* or address on some arcane aspect of the Torah, which orthodox rabbis are trained to do (at the drop of a hat, it would seem), Mason's drosh is on Jewish life in America.

He points out at the end of "Jackie Mason on Broadway" that he comes from a family of rabbis and that when he was one, he used to throw in a joke every once in a while to please his congregation. Then he threw in more jokes. Gentiles heard about him and started coming to his shul. Eventually, as he puts it, he was the only rabbi in America with a congregation that was all gentile. Then, he tells us, he started adding an entry fee and a minimum.

Jewish fools may like to have coffee and cake more than gentile ones (if Jackie Mason is right, that is) but they have played an important role in Jewish folklore in Europe and in American popular culture. A great deal of American humor (and maybe even American culture) has been Yiddishized due to the remarkable overrepresentation of Jews in the comedy world. Maybe, as a result of this, Americans are becoming more Jewish and, ironically, less foolish.

6

Mickey Mouse and Krazy Kat:
Of Mice and Men

Mickey Mouse is one of the most popular comic strip characters in the history of American popular culture (and popular culture all over the world, for that matter) and one of the most significant creations in animated films. What significance does this squeaky-voiced rodent have? What does he tell us about ourselves, our culture, our society, our ethos and mythos, our pathos and bathos—you name it? Why is this mouse such a monumental figure for pop culturists, mythologists, culture critics, and Disneyologists? These are some of the subjects I will explore in the chapter that follows.

A Mouse Involved With Technology

This report should be looked upon as a contribution to the study of mice in pop culture, a field to which I will give the neologism *mouse-ology*. It also deals with Disney and, since his work is so popular here, by implication, the American psyche. Here is how Walt Disney described Mickey's origin:

> His head was a circle with an oblong circle for a snout. The ears were also circles so they could be drawn the same no matter how he turned his head.
> His body was like a pear and he had a long tail. His legs were pipestems and we stuck them in big shoes [also circular in appearance] to give him the look of a kid wearing his father's shoes.
> We didn't want him to have mouse hands, because he was supposed to be more human. So we gave him gloves. Five fingers looked like too much on such a little figure, so we took one away. That was just one less finger to animate.
> To provide a little detail, we gave him the two-button pants. There was no mouse hair or any other frills that would slow down animation. (Schickel 1968,95)

This was necessary, so Richard Schickel explains in *The Disney Version* because Disney had to produce some 700 feet of film every two weeks; thus, he needed a character who was easy to draw.

We already see here the germ of Disney's passion—his fascination with technology and his willingness to let the requirements of machines dictate what he would do with his creations. It can be said that technology's inner necessities shaped Mickey Mouse, Disney's first significant creation, just as technological imperatives were to shape his other efforts, including Disneyland and Disneyworld. Mechanization already had taken command, decades before the idea of audio-animatronics had entered his head.

Freudian critics would, no doubt, feel compelled to speculate, at the very least, about the significance of Mickey Mouse's trying to wear his "father's shoes." Is there, we might ask, some kind of a hidden Oedipal aspect to this? And what about the symbolic castration—lopping off one of Mickey's fingers (on each hand) because five fingers looked like "too much" on a small character? Could these "birth traumas" be, in some way, connected to the sadism and cruelty one often finds in Mickey's actions (masked, of course, by a veneer of genial humor and nonsense)? And that squeaky voice of his? Is he one of the castrati?

The mouse is a familiar character in folklore and popular culture. There's a well-known tale about the mouse that gnawed through the ropes holding a lion, who had saved the mouse at an earlier time, and another tale about three blind mice, obviously not then castrated (even symbolically) who ran after a farmer's wife—with disastrous results. (I will not go into the messy details about this matter.) We've also had a Mighty Mouse figure, and, of course, that remarkable and magnificent mouse, Ignatz (hero of the brilliant comic strip *Krazy Kat*) about whom I'll have more to say later.

Mice are small, timid, dirty rodents with a passion, so we are told, for peanut butter and cheese. They have been anthropomorphized for centuries, but they have not always ended up as national heroes like Mickey Mouse, though to be fair, I would imagine that different media mice (as well as other creatures) have mirrored many of their cultures' dominant values and preoccupations as obediently and unobtrusively as he has.

It is hard to think that Mickey Mouse's great triumph in *Steamboat Willie* was in 1928, more than sixty years ago. Since that time he has been a character of some consequence and he, as well as his celebrated creator, "Uncle" Walt Disney, are worthy of considerable attention.

Mickey Mouse and the American Dream

The myth of America is that we can all be successful if we are willing to work hard enough. We can all emerge from the poverty and obscurity in which we are born and with a bit of luck, pluck, and virtue, reach a stage in which we can, like Benjamin Franklin (who is an important role model for us here) dine with kings. Or at least with movie stars and other showbiz celebrities. This is the American dream, which argues that social class is irrelevant and that individual willpower is the crucial factor in determining success.

There is, in the American psyche, a voracity, a hunger for experience, a lust (and I use the word with its sexual connotations in mind) for success and the symbols of success so that others will know that one is successful, that generates tremendous energy and dynamism, but also some other, less wholesome, consequences.

Disney was a small-town boy from the Midwest with all-American values. His life is a testimonial to the fact that some people, who are born in ordinary circumstances, can "make it." There seems little doubt, when you examine Disney's life and his work, that he was afflicted with a great and overwhelming desire to be a success, which might account, in part, for his well-documented compulsiveness. (It might also have something to do with his father, who was not a success by any means.) Much the same applies to Mickey Mouse, whose quest for experience seems Promethean or, at least, Kerouakian. Mickey's biography reads like something you might find on the dust jacket of a beat poet's book, describing his life and numerous occupations, travels, and adventures.

Here's Schickel's description of Mickey Mouse's career:

> The temporary solution to the problem of keeping Mickey fresh and amusing was to move him out of the sticks and into cosmopolitan environments and roles. The locales of his adventures throughout the 1930's ranged from the South Seas to the Alps to the deserts of Africa. He was, at various times, a gaucho, teamster, explorer, swimmer, cowboy, fireman, convict, pioneer, taxi driver, castaway, fisherman, cyclist, Arab, football player, inventor, jockey, storekeeper, camper, sailor, Gulliver, boxer, exterminator, skater, polo player, circus performer, plumber, chemist, magician, hunter, detective, clock cleaner, Hawaiian, carpenter, driver, trapper, whaler, tailor and Sorcerer's Apprentice. In short he was Everyman and the Renaissance Man combined,

a mouse who not only behaved like a man but dreamed dreams of mastery like all men. (1968, 117)

He was, then, a kind of homemade Leonardo Da Vinci—and like Leonardo, Mickey's sexual proclivities, and those of Walt Disney, his creator, are of considerable interest.

It is possible to argue that Disney had many personality traits associated with anal eroticism. In a celebrated essay of 1908 entitled "Character and Anal Eroticism," Sigmund Freud described anal erotics in the following terms:

> The persons who I am about to describe are remarkable for a regular combination of the three following peculiarities: they are exceptionally *orderly, parsimonious,* and *obstinate.* Each of these words really covers a small group of series and traits which are related to one another. "Orderly" comprises both bodily cleanliness and reliability and conscientiousness in the performance of petty duties. . . . "Parsimony" may be exaggerated to the point of avarice; and obstinacy may amount to defiance, with which irascibility and vindictiveness may easily be associated. (1963, 27–28)

These three characteristics are often connected with an eroticization of (and intense interest in) the anal zone.

Michael Brody, a psychiatrist, wrote an essay "The Wonderful World of Disney—Its Psychological Appeal," that discusses anality in Disney's work. (Ironically, this paper was delivered to a convention of psychiatrists at a meeting held at Disneyland.) Brody writes,

> The story of the two frivolous brother pigs and the contrasting hard-working pig [in "The Three Little Pigs"] chased by the hungry, big bad wolf, provides not only possibly a parable of the hard times of the early 1930's, but the virtues of obsessiveness. Plan, prepare, isolate and be orderly. Only the pig who builds a traditional house of brick saves the other two "silly pigs" from being eaten by the Big Bad Wolf.
>
> Anal themes are used defensively to lessen the anxiety of oral aggression, represented by the wolf's desire to eat the succulent pigs. . . . There is also the compulsive repetition in the story, going from house to house with the wolf and pigs saying the same phrase. This anality reaches its zenith when the wolf is punished by the huge mechanical spanking-machine. (1975, 2–3)

Brody points out that we find anal themes and messages in many other places in Disney, with the "often-kicked-in-the-butt Jiminey Cricket and the exaggeratedly buttocked Tinker Bell" (1975, 3), to cite a couple of other cases. Schickel says much the same thing. He writes, "Disney's interest in the posterior was a constant. Rarely were we spared views of sweet little animal backsides twitching provocatively as their owners bent to some task" (1968, 146).

Disney's anality really manifested itself in his great creations, Disneyland and Disneyworld. There, as Schickel puts it, Disney's "lifelong rage to order, control and keep clean any environment he inhabited" (1968, 15) could really take hold. He had "sanitized" the classics in his films— sometimes injecting anal resolutions to stories (as in the case of "The Three Little Pigs" cited above). This was one of the ways he "cleaned up" various stories (and "cleaned up" at the box-office as well, of course).

Beneath that folksy Uncle Walt exterior, beneath his pseudogeniality and amiability, strange forces were at work. Disney's need to control and manipulate would eventuate in Disneyland and Disneyworld (the latter the same size as San Francisco). In these parks, the ultimate in "clean" family entertainment, people could be (generally, without being aware of it) controlled, directed, and regulated. As Brody put it, "Disney strove for control over his work and destiny. What could be more natural than a huge, controlled playground where all could be Disney-regulated" (1975, 6). Employees in these parks attend training school for "smile and behavior regulation," and it is "control, not amusement, [that] seems the central theme in both the California and Florida parks" (1975, 6).

This marked a new development in Disney's desire for mastery and control. The very art form he chose to work in, animation, is one in which the creator has great control. You can make animated figures do whatever you want them to do. You don't have to worry about actors and actresses and other humans who may have minds and ideas of their own. As Schickel writes,

> Of course, for a man as intense as Disney in his desire to control his environment, animation was the perfect medium, psychologically. You can redraw a character, or even a line in his face, until it is perfect; you need never settle as the director of the ordinary film must, for the best an actor—imperfect human that he is—can give you. . . . Animation, to borrow from the unfortunate jargon of psychology, is a compulsive's delight. (1968, 161)

Thus, Disney progressed from animation to amusement parks, in his attempt to gain control over himself and others.

The ultimate move, for him, was the creation of those grotesque audio-animatronic figures. With them he does away with the vagaries of human personality and pushes the logic of control to its final and perhaps most absurd realization.

Disney also prided himself on the fact that Disneyland and Disneyworld were so immaculate. He is said to have come to Disneyland evenings to pick up litter that his sanitation workers had missed. What he created, his anti-septic wonderlands, were gum free, dirt free, and, it might be suggested, only slightly totalitarian. It may be, of course, that without recognizing it, Disney tuned into something buried in the psyches of his patrons—a desire to be controlled as a means, unconsciously of course, of dealing with their conflicts—pregenital and otherwise.

We must ask ourselves whether the various aspects of anal eroticism found in Disney struck some kind of chord buried deep in the American psyche or, at least, in the psyches of a large number of Americans. And others, all over the world, who are Disney fans, as well.

Children might find anal themes pleasant and take delight in barnyard humor. But what about adults who love Disneyland, the "happiest place on earth" (as it describes itself) and go there often? How do you explain the fact that many high schools celebrate proms at Disneyland? Does it provide a momentary regression or is there something other than regression involved (namely a kind of preconscious recognition of anxieties and personality problems)?

Krazy Kat—A Mouse to Admire

The mouse I love is Ignatz Mouse, George Herriman's malevolent, anti-authoritarian, incorrigible hero who heaved bricks at lovesick Krazy Kat for thirty years. The situation in *Krazy Kat* is complicated in the extreme. Ignatz loves throwing bricks at Krazy, who takes the bricks as signs of love. This is because thousands of years ago Kleopatra Kat was creased by a brick thrown by her lover and the memory has lingered on. Offissa Pupp, who loves Krazy and hates Ignatz, is the third major character. Pupp spends his life trying (in vain, generally speaking) to protect Krazy from Ignatz, and arresting him and throwing him in jail when he does crease Krazy with a brick.

We have, then, a mad and wonderful triangle of protagonists and antagonists and bricks. Ignatz is a brick-throwing menace who refuses to acknowledge the validity of authority and pays for his anarchistic, antisocial acts by spending a great deal of time in jail (separated from his wife and children, I might add).

There are, I would argue, two important themes in this strip: the triumph of illusion over reality (as shown by Krazy's belief that the bricks are signifiers of love) and antiauthoritarianism (as shown by Ignatz's brick throwing). Research I did a number of years ago suggests that Herriman was an African American who tried to pass for white, which would explain these two themes. I discussed this in my article "Was Krazy's Creator a Black Cat," *The San Francisco Examiner* (*This World Magazine*), 22 August 1971.

Ignatz is, in many respects, the opposite of Mickey Mouse and has infinitely more personality, spirit, and good humor. Mickey (like his creator) is so enterprising and so conventional, despite his frenetic behavior, that he becomes rather boring. That is why Disney felt trapped by Mickey and had to push him into a voracious quest for experience and find other characters, such as Donald Duck.

Ignatz, on the other hand, is an *autonomouse* character, who seldom fails to interest us and has cosmic as well as comic significance. I think Ignatz is an infinitely greater mouse, a more interesting mouse, and despite his anarchism, a much less threatening and dangerous mouse. Mickey represents, I suggest, pseudoindividualism and the illusion of freedom. Created to accommodate the necessities of mass production, designed to titillate the lowest common denominator, he now rules a "magic kingdom" in which human beings are, without their being aware of it, manipulated and controlled.

That Mickey Mouse is one of the most widely known heroes in the world of pop culture and entertainment is something I find troubling. The Disneyean worldview, as reflected by Mickey Mouse and Disney's other creations, including his amusement parks—compulsive, conservative (if not reactionary or even fascistic), entrepreneurial, mechanistic, and perhaps even sadistic (at times, at least) is not the only way of showing what this country stands for. Ignatz Mouse would be, to my mind, a much more representative and appealing representative hero. There is, of course, an element of compulsiveness in his behavior, too. He did, let us remember, spend thirty years throwing bricks at a poor, lovesick Krazy Kat and doing whatever he could to evade the rules and regulations of his society.

He was not a *Disneyfied* or even *dignified* character. But that, precisely, is his strength. And there was an element of playfulness and high spirits about his behavior that showed he was not really a victim of compulsions. If Mickey was the instrument of a "rage for order," then Ignatz was the instrument of a "love of disorder and chaos," of a messy world of wonderful, mixed-up characters. In the chart that follows I show the essential differences between these two characters:

Mickey Mouse	Ignatz Mouse
sadistic	playful
obedient	anarchistic
constrained	free
pseudoindividualistic	autonomouse
asexual	sexual
anal (reflects)	phallic

This chart suggests the differences between the two mice. I may have simplified things a bit, but I think it does a pretty good job of showing the dominant personality traits of each mouse and what each mouse reflects about his creator and his psychological makeup.

If Ignatz Mouse had a theme park, it would be considerably different and, I would imagine, a lot more fun than Mickey's. There certainly would be more of an opportunity to *do* things (as opposed to spectate, go on rides, etc.) and test one's skills, (at brick throwing, at the very least).

Final Thoughts

We are left with a problem. Does Disney's widespread popularity (in America and in many other lands, where Disney's characters are extremely well-known) reflect some kind of a camouflaged and diffused anality buried deep in our psyches? It has been argued by certain Marxist media critics that Disney's work champions bourgeois capitalist values and is, ultimately, an instrument of cultural imperialism. Is it possible that there is some kind of a connection between bourgeois values, capitalism, and anality? Is the anal personality type, then, one of the (if not *the*) basic personality types in modern capitalist societies, which would suggest, in turn, that Mickey Mouse is a symbolic figure who is truly representative? I tend to doubt this.

Let me explain why by pointing out a second consideration that Freud discusses relative to anal personality types. This has to do with the fact that, as Freud puts it, in "Character and Anal Eroticism,"

> The connections which exist between the two complexes of interest in money and of defecation, which seem so dissimilar, appear to be the most far-reaching. . . . In reality, wherever archaic modes of thought predominate or have persisted—in ancient civilizations, in myth, fairy-tale and superstition, in unconscious thoughts and dreams, and in the neuroses—money comes into the closest relation with excrement. (1963, 30–31)

There is, then, reason to believe that the character traits connected to anality by Freud—orderliness, parsimoniousness, and obstinacy—have a certain functionality in the modern world as far as making money is concerned but are also connected to archaic modes of thought—fantasies, myths, and so on.

Freud concludes his essay on anal eroticism by suggesting how people cope with anality in their lives, either by "unchanged perpetuations of the original impulses, sublimations of them, or by reaction-formations against them" (1963, 33). That is, some people (such as Disney) never abandon their anal personalities; some redirect the energy from their anality into other areas; and some turn against anality, and like a drunk on horseback, swerve over to opposite extremes.

I would like to think that most of us learn to outgrow our anality, though residues of it linger in our psyches and are sometimes activated. Disney's creations, like Mickey Mouse and Disneyland, do not help us deal with anal aspects of our personalities but, instead, reinforce this element in our psyches. Mickey Mouse is not like that mouse that gnawed the ropes constraining the lion in the folktale. Instead, Mickey Mouse, reflecting the unconscious elements in his creator's psyche, helps forge the chains that we use to bind ourselves.

7

Comics and Popular Culture: Not Just Kid's Stuff

A Note on Reading the Comics

If we look at comics in terms of the way they reflect cultural attitudes and values, there's more to them than meets the eye. Yet, for many years comics were seen as "kid's stuff." They were thought to be mere entertainments, relatively trivial matters that had no social significance and didn't deserve serious consideration or analysis by scholars or anyone else. In the past few decades, however, we have come to realize that the comics have more to them than we originally imagined. The term *comics* is a misnomer; many strips are not funny. They also do a wonderful job of reflecting social values and attitudes as filtered through the consciousness of the artists and writers who create them.

Most comic strip artists are simply trying to make a living by creating strips that people will like. They usually aren't aware that their work has any sociological or political relevance. Walt Kelly, whose strip *Pogo* satirized McCarthy and many other powerful political figures, argued that his work was pure fantasy and had no social or political meaning to it. I doubt that he actually believed that, but that was the pose that he struck. Many comic strip creators take the same position: "We're only trying to entertain people."

Artists and writers never are conscious of the full significance of what they are doing; this applies even to those who think they are (for example, Garry Trudeau, who draws *Doonesbury*) or the many underground comic book artists who have satirized American culture and society. That is why critics exist—to explain what artists and writers have done. Samuel Beckett was asked what the meaning of *Waiting for Godot* was. "If I knew," he replied, "I'd have told you."

Unlike films, radio programs, and television programs, comic strips and comic books are relatively easy to find and to analyze. They are a printed record covering more than ninety years of American history and are as close as the nearest library with microfilms or microfiches of local and regional newspapers, or comics store. And now there are many books about comics and collections of important comics, such as *Little Orphan Annie*, *Dick Tracy*, *Li'l Abner*, and *Superman*.

Analyzing the Comics

When we analyze comics, we consider their art style, narrative structure, and language. What values and beliefs are stressed? What attitudes do we find? Are certain groups stereotyped, and if so, what are these stereotypes like? Are allusions made to social and political matters? Are some groups underrepresented and others overrepresented? How, for example, are women, children, Latinos, blacks, Jews, Asians, and old people portrayed?

A look at some of our earliest strips shows that they were full of vicious stereotypes of members of minority groups. The artists who drew these strips were just reflecting commonly held attitudes and, no doubt, gave little thought to what they were doing. But stereotypes, sociologists suggest, have very powerful effects upon people—both on those who are stereotyped and those who participate in the stereotyping.

So the comics, though we may still think of them as "kid's stuff," are much more than that; they have played an important role in recording and perpetuating many deeply and commonly held beliefs and attitudes. It is only in recent years that minority and ethnic groups have had any success in attacking stereotyping, which still exists, especially when it comes to the way women are portrayed in the comics.

The First Generation of Comic Strips: The Innocents

Comic strips and comic books are quite different. I will deal with comics strips first, and then discuss comic books. American comic strips have passed through a number of different stages. Our earliest classic strips, such as *The Yellow Kid*, *The Katzenjammer Kids*, *Little Nemo*, and *Mutt and Jeff*, which came out in the 1920s, can be described as innocent. They tended to be humorous, light-hearted, and simple and probably are responsible for our notion that comic strips are childish fare. If we look beneath the humor, however, to what the strips revealed about American society, we find some interesting things.

The Yellow Kid and the Katzenjammer Kids

The Yellow Kid, for example, reflected an important theme in American culture—abandoned children, left to their own devices. This theme is connected to another one that plays an important role in the American psyche. Americans, it can be argued, are "spiritual orphans" who have abandoned their motherlands and fatherlands, to strike out on their own. They are free to create their futures, but the price they pay for this freedom is alienation and isolation. Sadly, the matter of abandoned and abused children still remains a problem in American society. What *The Yellow Kid* shows is that it is nothing new.

In *The Katzenjammer Kids*, Hans and Fritz are typical naughty boys, always stealing pies and playing tricks. This role is necessary to achieve male identities, since goodness and morality in American society tend to be associated with femininity. The kids, in constant conflict with their parents and with adults in general, are the focus of the strip. The comic provides an early reflection of generational conflict and child centeredness, two important American traits. Because the kids do not accept authority as valid, they don't internalize adult values and don't grow up; they also fail to deal with their aggressive feelings, except in childish ways.

The Second Generation of Comics Strips: The Modern Age Comics

The second generation of comics, what might be called the modern-age strips, included many of the classic American strips—*Krazy Kat, Little Orphan Annie, Dick Tracy, Buck Rogers, Blondie, Flash Gordon, Pogo*, and *Peanuts*. These strips are much more complicated. Some are humorous but many are not. And their subjects vary wildly, dealing with everything from a crime-obsessed detective battling a bestiary of grotesques to a little boy named Charlie Brown and his dog, Snoopy.

Little Orphan Annie: A Political Morality Tale

Although most of its readers probably didn't recognize it, *Little Orphan Annie* carried a strong ideological message. And why not? The comic strip, after all, is a kind of print medium that can support many different genres—action adventure, science fiction, domestic comedy and, in the case of *Little Orphan Annie*, a child-centered adventure story that camouflaged a political morality fable. Its story line reflected the ethos of the Coolidge era and championed the values of small-town America and big business.

In this strip, Daddy Warbucks (who grew to look more and more like Eisenhower) was a billionaire who befriended Annie. Warbucks was involved with an array of secret missions upon which the fate of the free world inevitably depended. Annie frequently complained that if businessmen like Daddy Warbucks were left alone and not hindered by governmental bureaucrats and red tape, things would be much better. Hers was a voice crying in the wilderness, for her values were out of sync with a modern, bureaucratized, urbanized America.

Dick Tracy

Dick Tracy, a very different kind of strip, told the story of a detective who battled (and conquered) dozens of criminal grotesques that came flooding out of Chester Gould's fertile imagination. The physical ugliness of these characters mirrored their moral ugliness, and provided an easy means of distinguishing the good guys from the bad guys.

Gould's style of cartooning also contributed to the morbidity and diffuse sense of terror in the strip. He used very strong blacks and whites, and, as a result, the strip's visual intensity captured the demonic nature of the characters and events in the stories. Tracy is a superego figure, par excellence. He reflects the sense of guilt and anxiety about evil that pervaded (and still pervades) American society and its popular culture. America, so this view suggests, is full of criminals and evil and every manifestation of this evil must be rooted out so our society can be made perfect. Tracy is one of a long line of avengers, who pursue evil with relentless energy and determination and who remind us that we must be eternally vigilant.

Blondie

If *Dick Tracy* was the archetypal procedural detective strip, *Blondie* was (and still is) the classic strip of domestic relations in America.

Dagwood is a representative figure in our popular culture, an "irrelevant" male. At one time, before he married Blondie, Dagwood was a playboy. But after his marriage, he quickly became a rather childish figure, often to be found trying to eke out a bit of comfort lying on the living room couch or raiding the refrigerator.

One of the conventions of American popular culture is that marriage is destructive of male authority—which explains why so many fathers in the comics and situation comedies are buffoons, whom nobody takes seriously. Dagwood Bumstead has no sex life (that we are aware of) and spends his life being abused by his boss and dominated by his wife and kids. And yet, despite his endless defeats and humiliations, he is cheerful and good-humored. He refuses to acknowledge his situation, and is unable to be truthful about his real feelings. It has been estimated that Dagwood wins in his various battles about 15 percent of the time, but you'd never know that from the way he acts.

Blondie is one of the most popular strips in American comicdom; it has been amusing us since 1930, though a new writer-artist team is doing the strip. Quite likely one of the reasons we like the strip is because it mirrors, in interesting ways, our lives—the relationships we have with our bosses, our spouses, and our children.

Many sociologists suggest that comics and other kinds of popular culture should be understood in terms of the uses they serve and the gratifications they provide people. From this perspective, *Blondie* is popular because, curiously enough, it helps us see ourselves more clearly. At the same time, in Dagwood it may be providing a role model for men that teaches them to avoid acknowledging their feelings by adopting a cheerful stance. That is how Dagwood copes, but it may not be the best way to deal with problems.

Peanuts

Although its message is far more sunny, *Peanuts* has its serious aspect. Created by Charles Schulz in 1950 (yes, it's been around for forty years), it deals with the experiences of a group of young children and a dog, Snoopy. These characters, such as Charlie Brown, Linus, Lucy, Shroeder, and Snoopy function as "naive commentators." Their passions mirror those of adults (who are never seen) and enable us to see our follies and crazy beliefs in a bit of perspective.

Schulz is a genial commentator on the human condition and uses Snoopy and all the other characters in *Peanuts* to poke fun at our behavior. There are several inversions in the strip: children act like adults and a dog acts like a human and is full of personality and spirit. The strip, like all comics, has changed over the years; Schulz's line is much more fluid, his characters' appearances have changed, and (especially in Snoopy's case) their personalities have developed and refined.

The characters in *Peanuts* are no longer mere comic strip figures: they have become part of our folk culture. Some scholars have also found a religious significance to *Peanuts* and a number of books and articles have been written on this aspect of the strip. Is there, in the background, these scholars ask, a diffused sense of guilt and a notion that humans are sinners? Foolish sinners, but sinners nevertheless.

American children now grow up reading *Peanuts*, cuddling Snoopy dolls, sleeping on *Peanuts* sheets, and surrounding themselves with images of its characters. And at the center of all this is Charles Schulz, a genial genius who read about an art school on a matchbook cover and sent away for information. The rest is history.

Doonesbury: The Voice of the Liberals is Heard in the Land

The last comic strip I would like to discuss is Garry Trudeau's *Doonesbury*. There is some debate about whether *Doonesbury* should be classified as a comic strip or as a political cartoon. Whichever it may be, *Doonesbury* deals very directly and consciously with social and political matters. Trudeau, a Yale- educated cartoonist, is merciless in the way he satirizes businessmen, celebrities, social types, and politicians—especially conservative politicians such as Ronald Reagan and George Bush. (He also attacks liberal politicians when he feels they deserve it.) His strips are both funny and savage—in the best tradition of a long line of comic strip artists, cartoonists, comedians, and other kinds of humorists, who have taken American politics and society as their subject.

Trudeau does not draw particularly well, but he has a brilliantly inventive mind. And like most humorists, he is a force that cannot be restrained whether by propriety or good sense. There is, in the great humorists (we saw it in *Krazy Kat* as well), a wildness and irreverence that shows no concern for traditional pieties. From time to time certain editors refuse to run *Doonesbury*, but Trudeau carries on and refuses to make compromises. This, it would seem, is the price we pay for having humorists. If they were able to restrain themselves, they probably wouldn't be humorists.

Humor can be a force for control and a force for resistance. In some cases, especially in small groupings, humor can coerce people into behaving in certain ways; in other cases, humor crystallizes popular opinion and strengthens the feelings people have that they should resist those with power. *Doonesbury*, I would say, is a force for resistance in American society. Trudeau satirizes and ridicules presidents, politicians, well-known personalities, and social practices and in many respects can be described as a spokesman for the liberal conscience in America.

There are countless other important strips that could have been discussed; we have created many strips since 1895, when *The Yellow Kid* appeared, and generations of Americans have grown up reading the comics in the newspapers. A look at strips from the 1930s and 1940s shows that they had larger dialogue balloons and used many more words. In recent decades, we have moved away from narrative strips to daily gag strips, since the comics can't compete very well with television when it comes to telling stories.

But the newspaper comic strip remains popular. Many Americans, adults as well as children, start off the day reading the comics. (President Reagan is alleged to have done so.) Then, with the "serious" reading of the day taken care of, they move onto the front page, the business section, or the sports section. We might only spend a few minutes each day on the comics, but when you add this up over the course of many decades, you can see that the comics play an important part in our lives.

Our attachment to the comics is so strong that during a newspaper strike in New York a number of years ago, the mayor read the comics over the radio so the citizenry wouldn't lose track of what was happening to its favorite characters.

Superman and the American Experience

We move now to a discussion of comic books and what they reflect about the American psyche and society. Comic books, magazines using the conventions of the comic strip (continuing figures, words in balloons, frames), got started in the 1930s. In 1935, *Popular Comics* appeared, which carried many newspaper strips. But in 1939 came the event that was to transform the comic book industry: *Superman* arrived. The adventures of the first of our caped crusaders were a great success and led to numerous imitators, such as *Captain Marvel* and *Batman*.

A look at the original two-page tale of *Superman* shows that he was born on a doomed planet, Krypton. He was sent off, alone, on a long, perilous voyage, in a small space ship, and eventually landed in America. A kindly old couple, the Kents, found the baby and adopted him. "The poor thing!—It's been abandoned," says Mrs. Kent. Even as a youth, Superman demonstrated superhuman powers, so his foster parents taught him to hide his strength (lest he scare people) and use it to assist humanity. When the Kents died, Clark Kent (Superman in disguise) decided to dedicate his life to "helping those in need."

This story, curiously, parallels the experiences of our Puritan forefathers. They, too, abandoned what they saw as a corrupt society, traveled in small vessels across a vast ocean to a new world where they had great power, and possessed a strong sense of mission. They feared corruption by the Old World, and their values—individualism, achievement, equality, the importance of willpower—have played an important role in American culture. Like Superman, they were conscience ridden, a trait that was instrumental in shaping the American psyche.

Although the parallels probably weren't intentional, Superman's personal code reflects the dominant values found in American society during the 1930s. Note also that Superman can only be weakened by exposure to Kryptonite—that is, a relic of his old world. For a long time, Americans had felt that European culture and values weakened and corrupted American ones, so the similarity is most interesting.

Superman has changed over the years. The first drawings were quite crude; later on, he become a very muscular and slickly drawn figure. And his powers increased, correspondingly—he flew, he had X-ray vision, and so on. Significantly, Clark Kent is a disguise. The mild-mannered, bumbling reporter is only a mask for the superhero hidden beneath.

This is, after all, a pose that many Americans adopt; underneath our facade of ordinariness is a heroic being just waiting for his big chance. There is, unfortunately, all too often a split between our dreams and our actual achievements. When we reach our thirties and forties, this disparity often leads to a sense of bitterness and depression over having failed, somehow, to show our true colors and achieve our goals.

The success of *Superman* led to the creation of Batman. He is yet another orphan who wars against crime, having seen his mother and father murdered by a vicious thug. Superman is a superpowerful alien; Batman is the disguise taken by Bruce Wayne, an aristocratic figure motivated by a desire for vengeance and a sense of noblesse oblige. He battles grotesque criminals, the most notorious of whom is the Joker, a pathalogical murderer with green hair, a chalk-white face, and an insane grin.

These grotesques help explain why it was possible for artists to forsake comedic spoofing (found in some episodes and in the television show, which was a campy satire) to dwell on Batman's dark side. This is reflected in the films and in recent booklength versions of *Batman* (*The Dark Knight*) and in new comic strip novels such as *Maus*. The comic strip medium is conducive to many different kinds of stories. Its heroes have moved from newspapers to magazines, ballets, musical comedies, films, and now to books. One of the reasons for this versatility is because the superheroes have become more three-dimensional.

Spider-Man and the Tormented Psyche

Stan Lee, the creator of *Spider-Man* and *The Fantastic Four* (and scores of other superheroes and superheroines) is probably the most influential writer of comics in recent years. His best known comic, *Spider-Man*, features Peter Parker ("Midtown High's only professional wallflower") who is bitten by a radioactive spider and becomes a super-hero with remarkable arachnoid powers.

What is remarkable about Spider-Man is that, compared to previous heroes, he is three-dimensional; he suffers from anxiety and guilt and often feels lonely and alienated. In an early episode he refuses to stop a thief who runs right by him. "From now on," he tells a policeman, "I just look out for number 1—that means—ME!" Because of his behavior, his uncle is killed by the thief. So Spider-Man learns, from this, that with great power comes great responsibility, and that failure to act often has negative consequences. He is, then, a much more believable figure. Many of Lee's other heroes were also rounded and humanized, and it was this innovation that made it possible for us to see comic book figures in a new way.

Ultimately, the humanization of the superheroes made it possible to make serious, full-length films about them. The success of the *Superman* films led to a film on Batman, which was an enormous commercial success, and to films about Popeye (based on an important utopian strip), Dick Tracy, and other heroes. We now are able to see these heroes (and there are, regrettably, relatively few heroines) as legitimate heroes, not as one-dimensional cartoon figures. Like all heroes, the superheroes are popular because they speak to our needs: they give us models to imitate and identify with, reflecting and reinforcing fundamental American beliefs and values.

Underground Comics and the New Wave Comic Artists

Heroes such as Superman and Batman are popular with many Americans. But there are a number of heroes and heroines who are found in strips and books who represent the opinions of critics of society and of various subcultures. The earliest of these counterculture comics were known as "underground" comics, and featured characters such as Mr. Natural, The Fabulous Furry Freak Brothers, and Trashman, to name just a few.

Mr. Natural and many other underground heroes satirized American middle-class culture as well as the fakery found in the counterculture. Their heroes reveled in "free" sexuality, a permissive attitude toward drugs, and antimilitarism; they displayed a comic revulsion toward politics and most aspects of American society. But underneath it all could be seen a kind of joyless and compulsive sexuality as well as a degrading attitude toward women, not to speak of a comedic nihilism. Robert Crumb, the creator of Mr. Natural, has been attacked for his sexism, but claimed (in a celebrated strip) the license of artistic freedom.

A newer generation of comic artists, a number of them women, has continued to satirize American politics and society, but in a more polished manner that is not designed to offend and outrage. These artists include Bill Griffith, who created *Zippy the Pinhead*; Matt Groening, whose weird characters "hellishly" satirize contemporary American society; Victoria Roberts, whose strip *Little Women* appears regularly in *Ms* magazine; and Gary Panter, whose character *Jimbo* inhabits a world devastated by nuclear bombs. These artists and many others use the comic strip form for telling commentaries on our values and beliefs, our fads and fantasies.

Traditionally we distinguish between cartoons, which are in single frames and have dialogue underneath, and comics, which have continuing characters, many frames and dialogue (generally) in balloons. The new-generation artists would all be classified as comic strip artists, but they do not always follow the genre's conventions. But neither did Herriman, for that matter. The younger cartoonists' work often appears in books as well as magazines and other periodicals.

Final Considerations on the Comics

It is hard to come to any conclusions about a body of work covering more than ninety years and created by thousands of artists and writers without resorting to glittering generalities. Still, if I were to choose one characteristic that seems central to American comic strips and comic books (and American culture) it would be our widespread antiauthoritarianism. We do not respect our so-called superiors and feel that authority is, generally speaking, not valid.

This is a heritage of our egalitarian value system; we may not have achieved an egalitarian society yet, but we are committed to doing so. In America we hold it to be self-evident that all men and women are created equal. The artists who create our comics often attack us for not doing a better job of realizing this goal. They do this by being satirical, by trying—and often succeeding—to outrage us through the use of pornography, and by championing (not always consciously, I might add) a general antiauthoritarian view of things.

All cultures carry on a dialogue with themselves, and there are American comic strip and comic book artists who attack the rebelliousness and antiauthoritarian motifs found in so many of our comics. Although strips such as *Dick Tracy* and *Little Orphan Annie* tend to support authority, "conservative" strips are few in number. Most of the time, social and political themes are invisible to the readers, who are merely looking for entertainment. But the themes reflected in comics do, in subtle ways, reinforce readers' values.

Heroes play an important role in our lives. We identify with them, we internalize their values, we try to imitate them. It has been suggested that the child is the father to the man. It is conceivable, then, that the heroes of our childhood and adolescence help shape our sense of self and society. Children and young adults read comics, collect them, and think a good deal about the adventures they have. So these paper heroes are much more important than we might imagine. When you know a person's heroes, you know a great deal about him.

Americans are not alone, of course, in having comic strips and comic books. There are brilliant comics in many countries; some, such as *Tintin* and *Asterix*, which are from Europe, are international favorites. And the comic book industry is an enormous one all over the world; most of the European countries publish a large number of magazines and books of comics. Disney's comics are widely read in Europe and South America, and have been attacked by Marxists, as a matter of fact, for spreading capitalist beliefs to unsuspecting readers. That, at least, is the thesis of a book called *How To Read Donald Duck: Imperialist Ideology in Disney Comics.*

UNESCO was involved with the publication of a book, *Comics and Visual Culture*, which dealt with comics in countries such as Japan, Kenya, Italy, America, Mexico, India, Russia, France and Britain. The study examined the way comics socialize young people—teach them values, beliefs, and roles. It found that comics tend to reflect the societies in which they are created and have an impact on people of all ages and social rankings.

In Japan, for example, hundreds of comic magazines, known as *manga*, are published each month. They are targeted to various groups, from young girls to adult males. More than ninety *gekiga*—erotic comic magazines—are published and they are widely read. There are also *songoku*, high-quality religious comics, and everything else in between. And Japan is but one of many countries with a flourishing comics industry.

In recent decades, sociologists and communications scholars have become increasingly interested in the comics. In Europe, Umberto Eco, the famous semiotician and novelist, has written extensively on the comics, and so have many other scholars. And there is a great deal of work going on in America, too. There are now many books about the comics and collections of important comics.

And who knows how many other remarkable new characters are being born in the imaginations of our writers and artists? They are about to join that pantheon of American comic strip and comic book heroes with whom we have grown up and who have merged into our lives, affecting them in ways that we are only beginning to understand.

8

Mark Russell in Buffalo

Mark Russell is a political humorist who has been a fixture on the American scene, and on public television, for a number of years. He makes amusing comments and sings witty songs about our politicians and the political scene in America. His style is genial and not biting; and he is strictly bipartisan. His purpose seems to be in pointing out what fools both Democratic and Republican politicians are—or perhaps, more precisely, what foolish things they have done. He also pokes fun at nonpoliticians as well.

In a recent appearance in Buffalo, shown on public television, he did the following:

1. Told a joke about Dan Quayle and a snowman.

2. Commented on the way members of the Salvation Army were being thrown out of some malls.

3. Told a joke about the Berlin Wall that involved souvenirs of the wall being made in Taiwan.

4. Joked about German tourists chopping off pieces of Leona Helmsley's hotel.

5. Told a Nancy Reagan astrologer joke, in which the astrologer said the Berlin wall would only be torn down when a black governor was elected in Virginia.

6. Spoofed George Bush's laid-back style and timidity. When asked about the Berlin Wall coming down, Bush refused to commit himself to anything saying, "We'll have to see what happens."

7. Sang a song about West Germany and East Germany uniting with references to "Deutschland über alles."

8. Joked about reports and surveys showing that young Americans are culturally illiterate, ignorant, and selfish.

9. Commented on the changes in the world—without anyone to hate, now, it doesn't seem like Christmas, he suggested.

10. Joked about the "Peace Dividend," the money we will be saving by cutting down on military purchases. With military hardware you can see where the money was wasted, he pointed out, while cash payments to HUD (Housing and Urban Development) contractors and consultants just disappeared.

11. Spoofed the conference between Bush and Gorbachev in Malta.

12. Sang a song about New York City being owned by the Japanese.

13. Suggested, mockingly, one eight-year term for the president and congressmen, to cut down on corruption that was so rampant in the 1980s.

14. Alluded to the Lincoln Savings and Loan scandal and the five "Keating" senators.

15. Joked about the television commercials being made by former Speaker of the House of Representatives Tip O'Neill and former Secretary of State Al Haig.

16. Sang a long roundup song about the 1980s that dealt with many of the major events, crises, and scandals in American politics: the Abscam bribes, inflation, the hostages in Iran, the Grenada invasion, bombing Libya, the Iceland summit, the Iran-Contra hearings, the Bork hearings, Dan Quayle, scandals involving Ed Meese and Jim Wright, the John Tower hearings, etc.

17. Told a Quayle joke. "If you have an A average in law school, you can become a judge; if you have a C average, you can become a corporate lawyer; and if you have a D average, you can become vice president of the United States of America."

In thirty minutes, Russell managed to mention a significant number of political events that once traumatized the country. A few years later, curiously, many of them were matters that we could laugh about. Russell, like many other humorists, uses allusion a great deal. His humor is based on common understandings and feelings people have about political events. Thus, a mere reference to some embarrassing situation (such as the relationship between Nancy Reagan and an astrologer or the Lincoln

Savings scandal) provokes a kind of guilty and uncomfortable laughter in people.

We recall all of these events, but in a different frame of reference. And that is because, perhaps, many of them have been resolved (or are on their way to being resolved) and are now looked on in a more general way for what they reveal about human beings and the human condition.

Some of the references—such as to the Japanese buying up New York—deal with anxieties we have about our sudden feeling of powerlessness and fears we have about our future. Humor has long been used as a coping mechanism and the allusion to the Japanese is a means of our expressing our fears and our hostilities. In these cases, our laughter is often "nervous," and points to problems that we find vexing and don't know how to deal with.

The laughter about the Japanese is really a way of dealing with our sense of weakness and, from the perspective I've been using, a means of retaliation. Much of Russell's humor has that function. We laugh at people, like Tip O'Neill and Al Haig, who were powerful and influential and now have become hucksters who make big money off of their names and former statuses. We also laugh at Russell's parody of Bush's noncommittal style—but this laughter is tied to questions we have about his personality and, in particular, about his ability to be a strong president. Bush's style of speaking, which reflects his cautiousness, has become the subject of a number of parodies by humorists in all media.

We also have to feel, collectively, somewhat shameful about the cultural illiteracy and shocking ignorance of so many of our young people; any indictment of the young, of course, indicts the adults who shape society and its institutions and give young people their values and ideals. So much of our laughter at Mark Russell's gibes and comments is a kind of "guilty" laughter. This is because it is we, the American people, who made possible or facilitated, through our gullibility, our self-centeredness and our lack of interest, much of what happened.

I should point out, also, that very little of Russell's humor comes from telling jokes—stories with punch lines. There were hardly any jokes, such as the Quayle joke at the end of the show, and the punch line there alluded to Quayle's deficiencies as a student and the questionable circumstances connected with his being admitted to law school. Many of Quayle's problems stemmed from his inept comments during the presidential campaign. A variety of gaffes and blunders in his speeches established him (or enabled the comedians to establish him) as a kind of "fool" figure. Since the campaign, the comedians and jokesters have created many Quayle jokes. Comedians only have to mention his name now to elicit laughter.

In dealing with political humor, one must always raise the question of the ultimate result of all the jokes and satires that humorists make. Does humor of resistance actually do anything? Are those in power affected in any significant way by this humor? Or is this humor irrelevant? And perhaps even dysfunctional? We may get psychological gratifications from humorous "attacks" on those in power that serve as a substitute for becoming politically active or that give us the illusion that we are, somehow, getting back at them. We laugh at those in power ("that'll teach them," we say to ourselves) and they make the laws and appoint Supreme Court justices.

On the other hand, it may be that this humor serves to make people pay more attention to what is going on in the political world, to be more critical of those in power, and to provide a sense of consensus that ultimately has an impact. The fact that dictators generally kill comedians as soon as they can makes me think that comedians actually do matter, and that the power of ridicule, of satire, of scornful laughter, is a great and a contervailing force to actual political power.

Personally speaking, I find Mark Russell's humor rather bland and tame. But comedians come in all shapes and sizes and ideologies, and they all have different styles and ways of operating. There is also the danger, with political humor, of seeming to be one-sided. Humorists who appear to be partisan immediately lose a good deal of credibility with many members of the opposition, in our case, the party under attack. The routine is then seen as essentially political and only secondarily humorous.

So American political humorists have to be careful to deal with politics, in general, and be bipartisan in their attacks on the foibles, inanities, and crimes perpetrated by our politicians. There are, of course, humorists and comedians who do have very well-defined political beliefs and ideologies, many of whom are liberal or even radical. And they have the advantage, often, of "preaching to the converted" when they appear in clubs or rallies or create their comic books and comic strips.

Political humorists such as Mark Russell (or Art Buchwald) find themselves in a somewhat difficult situation in that they cannot let political convictions get in the way of their being humorists. As such, they have to deal with politics in terms of how it is a reflection of the human condition and its numerous frailties, weaknesses, and depravities. This leads to a more whimsical, friendly kind of humor, that pokes fun rather than excoriates our politicians.

The irony that most political humorists have to deal with is that they can't be too political. But even within these parameters, a great deal can be done. Russell's comedy show, genial as it was, showed that both of our political parties (and American society, in general) have a great deal to be embarrassed about. And so do we, the American people. We laughed (as is often the case) so we wouldn't have to cry.

9

A Cool Million

A Cool Million, by Nathanael West, is an exasperating novel. It deals with an issue that is central to the American consciousness—the self-made man—but it does so in such a zany manner that it is hard to take the novel seriously. It is a brilliant parody of the Horatio Alger myth, which was just dying out in the 1930s. It may not be an artistic success but it does deal with matters of considerable significance, and, in particular, reflects the fear that fascism, draped in the American flag, might develop in America.

Every adventure of its hero, Lemuel Pitkin, ends in disaster and the novel finally concludes with Pitkin being murdered, after having been "dismantled" during the course of his pathetic attempts to become a success, in the classic American tradition of rising from rags to riches.

West becomes so intoxicated by his bag of tricks and is so fixated on the importance of his message that he turns the novel into a melodramatic series of slapstick adventures, full of caricatures that we cannot take seriously. And yet, by giving his characters a symbolic dimension, he does find a way to spread his message, even if we can't identify emotionally with them. West isn't dealing with human beings but, instead, a myth—the so-called American Dream—and he attacks this myth by perverting and reversing it.

The immense irreverence of *A Cool Million* is disconcerting to most readers; West takes something sacred to most Americans, our sense of possibility, and rides it mercilessly, pointing out how illusory it is and demonstrating its tragic impact on the American consciousness and on American society.

For every self-made man or woman, who has become rich and successful in America, there are legions who have not and who feel, therefore, that they are failures. Written at the height of the Great

Depression, in 1934, *A Cool Million* is a pessimistic and cynical view of American culture and society.

The dismantling of the hero, Lemuel Pitkin, is symbolic of the social degeneration that West believed pervaded American life. And his nightmare ending, which shows America being taken over by Fascists masquerading as super-Americans, was something many people were afraid might happen during the early years of the Great Depression. It was feared that the country would swerve radically toward either the Left or the Right—until the New Deal came along to save the country. Ironically, the New Deal was once considered a radical movement; now it is generally considered to be a conservative one, one that saved Capitalism.

A Cool Million is the story of a poor, but honest, farm boy, Lemuel Pitkin, who goes out into the world to seek his fortune—in the best American tradition. He is urged (and forced) to do this by one Shagpoke Whipple, a former president of the United States and the owner and president of the Rat River National Bank. Whipple encourages Pitkin in the following words:

> "America," he said, with great seriousness, "is the land of opportunity. She takes care of the honest and industrious and never fails them as long as they are both. This is not a matter of opinion, it is one of faith. On the day that Americans stop believing it, on that day will America be lost."
> "Let me warn you that you will find in the world a certain few scoffers who will laugh at you and attempt to do you injury. They will tell you that John D. Rockefeller was a thief and that Henry Ford and other great men are also thieves. Do not believe them. The story of Rockefeller and of Ford is the story of every great American, and you should strive to make it your story. Like them, you were born poor and on a farm. Like them, by honesty and industry, you cannot fail to succeed. (1965, 15)

The book amounts to a savage ridiculing of the various elements of the American way of life and what we might call "the American imagination." It is a veritable hatchet job on such aspects of American mythology as the *innocent* American girl, the loudmouth westerner (known as *the ring-tailed roarer*), American taste, Wall Street, spies, Southern lynch mobs, anarchists, and hero worship. Much of the humor in the book is based on West's ravaging of our myths in an attempt, one must presume, to make us see our situation in more realistic terms.

Thus, the heroine of the story, Betty Prail, does not keep her virtue very long. She is raped by the town bully, Tom Baxter, and then by two Italian white slavers (who carry her off to a whorehouse in New York), and is had by everyone who can get his hands on her, until she ends up, finally, as Whipple's "secretary." This is a mockery and ridiculing of the convention of feminine innocence in American girls, especially small-town girls.

The whorehouse that Betty ends up in is one of West's most brilliant bits of satire. He incorporates in his satire, to great advantage, such techniques as cataloguing, stereotyping, and theme-and-variation.

Wu Fong, the owner of the whorehouse, prides himself on his international style, and has girls from every country—but he lacks a good American girl to round out his collection:

> The reader may be curious to know why he wanted an American girl so badly. Let me say now that Wu Fong's establishment was no ordinary house of ill fame. It was like that more famous one in the Rue Chabanis, Paris, France—a "House of All Nations." In his institution he already had a girl from every country in the known world except ours, and now Betty rounded out his collection. (1965, 31)

The house is fitted out with each suite decorated to the style of each girl's country of origin. However, when the depression hits, Wu Fong is forced by the Hearst "Buy American" campaign to go American 100 percent, and so redecorates along American motifs.

In the passage that follows, West satirizes American regional motifs and styles:

> Lena Haubengrauber from Perkiomen Creek, Bucks County, Pennsylvania. Her rooms were filled with painted pine furniture and decorated with slip ware, spatter ware, chalk ware, and "Gaudy Dutch." Her simple farm dress was fashioned of bright gingham.

> Alice Sweethorne from Paducah, Kentucky. Besides many fine pieces of old Sheraton from Savannah, in her suite there was a wonderful iron grille from Charleston whose beauty of workmanship made every visitor gasp with pleasure. She wore a ballgown from the Civil War period.

West lists nine different girls and describes their suites in the same detail. The mock seriousness of his concern for style and consistency contrasts greatly with the "low usage" to which these girls and the interior decorating is to be put.

Rabid Americanism appears periodically throughout the book, especially in the oratory of Whipple. At first glance Whipple seems to be the most important villain in the story; he mouths the platitudes Americans are all familiar with and he eventually leads a takeover of the country by Fascists. But Whipple is only the personification of perverted American ideas and ideals, and it is these that West suggests are the real villains in the story. Whipple is an ideologue, a true believer who, in the name of patriotism, does horrible things—and with a passionate intensity, since he believes in the superior morality of his ideas and his actions.

West makes Whipple ludicrous in an effort to show how absurd his ideas are; but he is, nevertheless, West suggests, dangerous. Whipple's advice to Lemuel Pitkin is straight out of Horatio Alger:

> America is still a young country...and like all young countries it is rough and unsettled. Here a man is a millionaire one day and a pauper the next, but no one thinks the worse of him. The wheel will turn, for that is the nature of wheels. Don't believe the fools who tell you that the poor man hasn't got a chance to be rich anymore because the country is full of chain stores. Office boys still marry their employers' daughters. Shipping clerks are still becoming presidents of railroads. Why only the other day, I read where an elevator operator won a hundred thousand dollars in a sweepstakes and was made a partner in a brokerage house. Despite the Communists and their vile propaganda against individualism, this is still the golden land of opportunity. (1965, 35)

These words were written when 10 million Americans were unemployed and the whole of American society was in turmoil. West thought he was attacking a myth and thought his novel would be a means of resistance against it. What is interesting is that Whipple's words still have resonance.

Even during the Depression, many Americans still felt that they were personally responsible for being out of work and for all the dislocations convulsing America. The dream was, and to some extent still is, more powerful than reality. If experience made a mockery of the American Dream, people were more ready to question their experiences rather than the dream. West, of course, ridiculed the American Dream and thought he was bringing people to their senses with his satirical brilliance.

It didn't matter, then, that Whipple shows himself to be a fool and spends a great deal of time mouthing silly platitudes and ridiculous indictments. He babbles about Wall Street working hand-in-hand with the communists, and lards his rhetoric with anti-Semitic comments. Whipple is financed by an oil-rich primitive and flourishes in the South, which has a long tradition of political demagoguery.

The book is so overblown and the characters are so stereotyped that we cannot take *A Cool Million* seriously as a work of art. Yet it does have a certain amount of value as a social document, perhaps as relevant today as when it was written.

The eulogy Whipple offers for Pitkin is remarkable:

> Of what is it that he speaks? Of the right of every American boy to go into the world and there receive fair play and a chance to make his fortune by industry and probity without being laughed at or conspired against by sophisticated aliens. (1965, 105)

America must be saved from sophistication and from aliens. (This conception, silly as it is, still has many adherents.) In the last part of the eulogy, Pitkin is shown to be a Christlike figure:

> But he did not live or die in vain. Through his martyrdom the National Revolutionary Party triumphed, and by that triumph this country was delivered from sophistication, Marxism and International Capitalism. Through the National Revolutions its people were purged of alien diseases and America has become again America. (1965, 106)

Pitkin, Whipple tells us, is an American Christ who dies that Americanism might live. With this sacreligious note, the novel ends.

West tried to use satire and humor as a means of shocking Americans and bringing them to their senses. He believed that he could make them see what, to him, was a privileging of illusions over reality, of dreams against experience. He feared that in the chaos of American life in the 1930s, there was a danger of America being taken over by right wing or Fascistic elements, selling themselves as super-Americans. He fought with the tools that he used best—satire, ridicule, absurdity. His political feelings tended to overwhelm his aesthetic sensibilities, so *A Cool Million* isn't really a success as a novel. Still, it is very funny and must reading for anyone interested in American humor and the way it relates to our values and beliefs.

10

Twelfth Night:
Comedic Techniques and Social Considerations

On Humorous Techniques

This study of humorous techniques in *Twelfth Night* is, first, meant to be seen as a very practical, down-to-earth, investigation of some of the methods Shakespeare used to generate laughter (and other related states of being such as mirth, amusement, elation, call it what you will) in his play. It is an application of the techniques of humor that I have listed and explained in my glossary and is meant to reveal some of the devices Shakespeare employed in *Twelfth Night*.

By focusing on techniques I believe I can demonstrate how Shakespeare created his humor and explain why it is that we still find Shakespeare so funny. I can recall seeing a recent production of *Twelfth Night* that was simply side-splitting. My focus, then, is not on themes or philosophical matters relating to the nature of comedy, the human psyche, or that kind of thing, but on the nuts and bolts of generating humor. I will also deal with other matters such as the way the play reflects social and political beliefs.

The Matter of Performance

I do not wish to deal with this important matter at any length here, but I would like to say something about performance. My glossary does not deal directly with performance qualities nor the powers that actors and actresses have to use voice intonation, body language, facial expression (among other things) in the service of comedy. (Performance is covered indirectly in my category of humor involving action or visual and nonverbal elements of humor.)

Obviously, people who attend a comedy at a theater come predisposed to laugh and be amused. But acting and production qualities are extremely important in generating that "willing suspension of disbelief" that is, we are told, so important to the experience of theater. Let us assume, then, that any production of *Twelfth Night* we might be attending is well acted and well directed, and take all of this as a given. It is possible, of course, for great performers to transcend (to varying degrees) mediocre or bad plays. But with great plays, such as *Twelfth Night*, and great performances and production values, the job is immeasurably eased and the pleasure is greater.

My focus, then, will be on the written play and the numerous devices found in this dramatic work that *make* people laugh. The fact that we are often powerless (an important word to keep in mind) to resist laughing suggests that there is an element of coercion involved in great comic drama and theater. There is, if you think about it, something funny about being *made* to do something (laugh) that we desperately want to do—which is why we read the play or went to see it performed in the first place. In this respect, laughter is a two-edged sword. It can be used by those in power, or those who accept their view of things, to force acquiescence. But it also can be used by those out of power to resist domination.

Chris Powell, a sociologist, believes that humor is an instrument of social control by dominant elements in society; that is, humor always represents their perspective on things. As he writes in "A Phenomenological Analysis of Humour in Society,"

> The ultimate control is, in fact, the view we hold of social reality and our understanding of our own and other people's place within it, including our resistance to the actions and beliefs of others we dislike and repudiate. Life consists essentially of constantly negotiating our understandings with other people. . . . It can be suggested that humour plays a fundamental role in these negotiations. (1988,99)

There are, in all societies, differentials of power and Powell argues that humor is used to reinforce the acceptance of the beliefs of those who are at the top of the pyramid. He mentions how superordinates often tell jokes and subordinates feel constrained to laugh at these jokes (even when they are directed at themselves). As he writes,

> Invariably what is reinforced though this form of humour, and rarely challenged, is a dominant ideological position. One could go further and assert that, in any given

society, humour is a control resource operating both in formal and informal contexts to the advantage of powerful groups and role-players. (1988,100)

If Powell is correct, humor is a subject that demands a considerable amount of attention by sociologists and political scientists as well as psychologists and literary theorists, for it is a useful guide to the dominant beliefs found in a given society. It enables us to "read" the dominant ideologies of the day.

Powell recognizes that this dominant ideology is challenged at times, but he downplays the significance of these instances of resistance. From this perspective, humor is tolerated (maybe even encouraged) since it is a means of societal tension-relief; it enables people to let off steam. Others would give the resistance aspects of humor more significance. Humor, for example, can undermine the authority and legitimacy of elites or members of elites (for example Quayle jokes in America) by suggesting that they are stupid—the ultimate putdown in an information society. Other elite figures (Bush, Trump, etc.) are ridiculed for a variety of other reasons, as a glance at *Doonesbury* demonstrates. Boss Tweed, it has been suggested, was destroyed by being ridiculed in Nast's cartoons. What effect *Doonesbury* or Johnny Carson has had on the political scene is another question.

In any case, there is good reason to argue that humor tells us a great deal about social and political matters, even though a play, such as *Twelfth Night*, or any other text might not be directly concerned with these matters.

The Title: *Twelfth Night: or, What You Will*

The title of the play alludes to revelry and pleasure.

And the subtitle is somewhat bewildering in that it suggests readers will be allowed to make their own interpretations, to make whatever sense they can, of the play. There is a kind of latitude and openness that is slightly disquieting. Is there, we might ask, no official or prescribed meaning to the text?

The audience is asked to enter into the process here and make whatever sense it can of the proceedings. Could Shakespeare have anticipated the *reader-response* school of criticism which argues that readers are almost equally involved as authors in the creation of literary works? His subtitle certainly suggests his thinking was in this vein. This implies a new relationship between authors and readers, a more democratic (if you will) sense of things.

This is what Wolfgang Iser argues in "The Reading Process: A Phenomenological Approach." He writes,

> The literary text activates our own faculties, enabling us to recreate the world it presents. The product of this creative activity is what we might call the virtual dimension of the text, which endows it with its reality. This virtual dimension is not in the text itself, nor is it in the imagination of the reader; it is the coming together of text and imagination. (Lodge 1988, 215)

There are gaps, Iser suggests, in all texts. Different readers fill in the gaps in different ways, which is why all texts are inexhaustible. In essence, all texts depend on their readers (and performers) who, one might say, enter into partnerships with the writers to fully realize a given text. Shakespeare seems to have understood this when he gave the play its subtitle. Make of it what you will, he suggested. (Whether there are preferred readings of texts is a complicated matter which literary theorists are debating. All readers may be equal, but to play on Orwell's famous line, some readers are, or may be, more equal than others.)

The Names of the Characters

A look at the names Shakespeare gives his characters tells us, immediately, that we are going to be following the adventures of a variety of zanies and comic grotesques. We have characters named Aguecheek (ague being a kind of fever), Toby Belch (a belch being an indiscreet and generally involuntary noise coming from the stomach), and Malvolio. A good case can be made for this name being a slight modification of the Italian *malvolere* or "bad will." *Volio* is very close to the Italian *voglio* which means "I want." Malvolio would mean, then, something "bad willed" or not wanted. Feste, as in festival suggests pleasure and joy and is rather direct.

Orso means "bear," and the suffix *ino* means "little," so Duke Orsino is "little bear." He is the only person among the elevated and normal characters in the play with a comic name. All of the other names of important characters are ordinary. Interestingly, the use of comic names does not divide along class lines, for we have *Sir* Toby Belch and *Sir* Andrew Aguecheek; giving these characters titles only heightens the humor. The names of many of the characters are, then, comic and are indicators of their comic personalities. But even those characters without comic names often find themselves in ridiculous situations.

On Practical Jokes

One of the major scenes in the play involves Malvolio finding a forged letter that he believes has been written by the woman he serves, Olivia. It is written in an ambiguous manner that allows Malvolio to read all kinds of things into it. It reads as follows:

> If this fall into thy hand, revolve. In my stars I am above thee; but be not afraid of greatness: some are born great, some achieve greatness, and some have greatness thrust upon 'em. Thy Fates open their hands; let thy blood and spirit embrace them; and, to inure thyself to what thou art like to be, cast thy humble slough and appear fresh. Be opposite with a kinsman, surly with servants; let thy tongue tang arguments of state; put thyself into the trick of singularity: she thus advises thee that sighs for thee. Remember who commended thy yellow stockings, and wished to see thee ever cross-gartered: I say, remember. Go to, thou art made, if thou desirest to be so; if not, let me see thee a steward still, the fellow of servants, and not worthy to touch Fortune's fingers. Farewell. She that would alter services with thee.
>
> THE FORTUNATE UNHAPPY (Act 2, scene 5)

This letter, written in an ambiguous manner and in the hand of Olivia, is what we would now describe as a practical joke.

Martin Grotjahn, a Freudian psychiatrist, discusses these jokes in *Beyond Laughter*:

> The practical joke represents a primitive form of the funny which is often so cruel and so thinly disguised in its hostility that the sensitive or esthetically minded person can hardly enjoy it. The practical joke is a dangerous performance, a realization of the sadistic and often cruel tendency which underlines the creation of wit. (1966,40)

Of course, in the play, Malvolio is a rather unpleasant person who is full of himself, so that we delight in his being brought low, but there is an obvious element of aggression and hostility that Grotjahn mentions that shows in this scene. The comic frame of the play minimizes the practical joke somewhat, for the comedy has already established an ambience of nonsense and foolishness that helps cushion the hostile intent behind the joke. And like many practical jokes, Malvolio's discomfiture turns serious and he is made to suffer considerably.

Mistakes and Mistaken Identities

I make a distinction in my glossary between *mistakes* (something one does, an action, that is in error, that is incorrect) and *misinterpretation* (which involves not interpreting or understanding a statement correctly). Malvolio mistakenly thinks the letter he finds is from Olivia. This is because the handwriting on the letter is similar to that of Olivia's, though we readers (or members of the audience) know that the letter is a forgery. He also misinterprets it.

In one of Shakespeare's classic bawdy scenes, Malvolio examines the letter and concludes, from looking at the handwriting, that it was written by Olivia. He says:

> By my life, this is my lady's hand: these be her very C's, her U's and her T's: why that? (Act 2, scene 5)

Her *C*'s, *U*'s and (*N*) *T*'s is a very direct and vulgar reference to Olivia's vagina and reveals both his desires and, indirectly we may surmise, the rather reductionist way he thinks of her. Malvolio's mistake leads to his bizarre behavior, which is, in turn, mistaken by others as that of a madman. Consequently, Malvolio is incarcerated.

We might also wonder whether there is a subtext in the play—whether Malvolio's lamentable fate is meant to show the folly of trying to rise above one's station. In this respect, he serves as an example of a person with both personal and social hubris who comes to ruin because of his ambition. There is a conservative element here, one that suggests that the status quo must be maintained. It is covered over by all the nonsense surrounding Malvolio and his personality, but his comic demise also can be read as a cautionary tale. He himself seems to believe that only luck (fortune) can elevate him. "T'is fortune, all is fortune," he says, believing somehow that a miracle has happened. Without fortune, we may presume, people are destined to stay at whatever level they find themselves on the great chain of being.

The other important mistake involves not class but gender. Viola has disguised herself and taken on a male identity, that of a youthful page, Cesario. This leads, ultimately, to all kinds of crazy complications. Viola, pretending to be Cesario, is employed by Duke Orsino. He is madly in love with Olivia, who can't stand him. Orsino sends Cesario (that is, Viola) to woo Olivia in his name, and she promptly falls in love with

Cesario. Meanwhile, Cesario (that is, Viola) has fallen in love with Orsino. Viola speculates on this crazy turn of events:

> Disguise, I see, thou art a wickedness,
> Wherein the pregnant enemy does much.
> How easy it is for the proper-false
> In women's waxen hearts to set their forms!
> Alas, our frailty is the cause, not we!
> For such as we are made of, such we be.
> How will this fadge? my master loves her dearly;
> And I, poor monster, fond as much on him;
> And she, mistaken, seems to dote on me . . .
> O time! thou must untangle this, not I;
> It is too hard a knot for me to untie!
> (Act 2, scene 2)

It is how this mixup is resolved that is the central problem of *Twelfth Night*. And it is through another mistake—when Olivia sees Viola's twin brother Sebastian, and marries him (thinking she is marrying Cesario) that the knot is able to be unraveled.

The fact that so much of the humor in *Twelfth Night* revolves around these mistakes indicates that logical humor plays an important role in the play. (Logic is one of the four basic categories that I discussed in my glossary.) Malvolio makes a mistake about who wrote the letter he found (because he was fooled by the handwriting) and most of the characters in the play mistakenly believe Viola is a youthful male, Cesario.

It might also be suggested that the matter of identity is at the heart or core of the play. One can argue that the forged letter involves the technique of imitation (of the handwriting), which is humor of identity. Other examples are Viola impersonating a male, and the scenes involving Viola's twin brother, Sebastian. So, a central element of the play involves mistaken identity.

Sir Andrew Aguecheek also makes a mistake involving identity. He is tricked into a fight with Cesario but comes to grief when he ends up fighting (not realizing who he is dealing with) Sebastian. Sir Andrew is a classic "gull" who is so naive that he believes the most fantastic things people tell him—that he has a chance to win Olivia's hand, for example. This might be classified as a mistake but is closer to a different matter, revelation of ignorance and gullibility, which is part of the humor of logic.

One of the problems with a classification system such as the one I've made is that often there are a number of different techniques of humor operating at the same time and sometimes it is difficult to determine which technique is fundamental. How do we make sense out of the humor involving Viola's impersonation, or mistaken identity? Is it the mistake which is central (humor of logic) or the identity (humor of identity)? This has to be determined, I would suggest, on a case by case basis.

When Olivia falls in love with Cesario many different things are happening, as far as our perception of humor is concerned. Obviously, she has made a mistake, for she thinks Cesario is a male while we, the readers (or members of the audience) know Cesario is really a woman, Viola, who is impersonating a male. Olivia is, in a sense, a victim. Ironically, the person who finds the notion of loving the Duke quite impossible becomes involved in a really impossible situation. This might be understood as an example of reversal except that it is not a person but the fates that equalize things. We find it amusing that this headstrong woman can become such a fool as to fall in love with another woman, in the context of the conventions of the age and the theater of the time, that is. In modern society, the notion of a woman falling in love with another woman is not terribly surprising, though we must remember that Olivia thinks Cesario is a male.

Unmasking and Revelation

Given that identity is a central concern in the play, it is only natural to expect to find that unmasking and revelation are of major importance as well. Malvolio is, we're told, very taken with himself and has delusions about his importance and his possibilities. Thus, Maria tells us in act 2, scene 2, that Malvolio has spent a half-hour in the sun "practicing behavior to his own shadow."

Malvolio believes he is fortune's darling. As he says, "T'is fortune, all fortune." He reveals his fondest dream—becoming Count Malvolio by marrying Olivia and it is at this moment that he finds the fake letter and is told, "Be not afraid of greatness." Thus, Malvolio has puffed himself up horrendously and is ripe for having his balloon pricked. It is his megalomania that makes his victimization so delicious.

When Malvolio follows the instructions in the letter, he reveals his gullibility and is turned into a clown who is, in turn, mistaken for a madman. On the basis of the letter, he misinterprets Olivia's statement in act 3, scene 4. He has mentioned that he doesn't feel well and she asks, "Wilt thou go to bed, Malvolio?" He replies, misinterpreting her question, "To bed! aye, sweet-heart, and I'll come to thee." When he is asked about his ridiculous boldness in front of his lady, he quotes the letter, "Be not afraid of greatness," and other lines to Olivia, but she doesn't know what he is talking about and concludes he has "midsummer madness."

Malvolio's mistake (about the author of the letter) leads to his bizarre behavior and his misunderstanding of Olivia's behavior. In turn, his behavior is mistaken for that of a madman and he is incarcerated. Malvolio is attacked because, among other things, he offends others, who want to get back at him and know they can do so because of defects in his personality.

Absurdity, Confusion, and Nonsense

It is the triangle of mistaken or, more properly, misdirected loves that is at the heart of the play. The Duke loves Olivia, who cannot stand the sight of him. Olivia loves Cesario, who is a woman pretending to be a man. And Cesario loves Orsino. Everyone loves someone who loves someone else.

The play is about the resolution of this absurdity and the confusion generated by Viola's disguise and the fact that she has an identical twin brother, Sebastian. There is something pleasing, it seems, about untangling a mess and having everything come out well at the end, especially when the matter of romantic love is involved.

Comedic Techniques in Twelfth Night

In this chart I will list some of the main techniques of humor used in *Twelfth Night* and identify one or two examples where they are used. This will show the range and variety of techniques Shakespeare used.

1. *Mistakes*
   The practical joke on Malvolio by Maria
   Olivia loving Cesario (Viola) who loves Orsino
   Aguecheek attacking Sebastian, thinking him to be Viola
2. *Unmasking and Revelation*
   Malvolio's pretensions
   Viola's disguise
3. *Absurdity, Nonsense, and Confusion*
   Triangle of lovers, each loving someone else

      The duel between Aguecheek and Viola
4. *Impersonation*
      Viola impersonating a page, Cesario
5. *Irony*
      Viola saying "I swear I am not that I play." (Act 1, scene 5)
      Viola telling Olivia "I am not what I am." (Act 3, scene 1)
6. *Bombast or Inflated Speech*
      Malvolio's "Greatness" speech
7. *Insults and Degradation*
      The practical joke on Malvolio
      Maria describing Aguecheek as a "fool" and coward
          (Act 1, scene 3)
      Malvolio calling a clown a "barren rascal"
      The practical joke on Cesario (the duel)
8. *Facetiousness*
      "For what says Quinapalus? 'Better a witty fool than a
          foolish wit." Mock learning shown in statement
          by the clown.
      "I am indeed not her fool, but her corrupter of words."
          Statement by clown. (Act 3, scene 1)
9. *Overliteralness*
      Response of clown when questioned by Viola.
          "Dos't thou live by thy tabor?" "No, sir, I live
          by the church."
10. *Ignorance, Gullibility, and Naiveté*
      When Maria tells Sir Andrew Aguecheek, "Bring your
          hand to the buttery bar" (to flirt) he doesn't understand.
11. *Comic Definitions*
      Duke's definition of lovers: "Unstaid and skittish. . . . "
          (Act 2, scene 4)
12. *Misunderstanding*
      Duke's and Cesario's discussion of "his" ideal lover
          (Act 3, scene 4)
      Viola's statement: "I am all the daughters of my father's house."
          (Act 2, scene 4)
      When Olivia says, "Wilt thou go to bed, Malvolio?"
          he thinks she wants to make love with him.
13. *Wordplay*

Viola's aside " . . . a little thing [penis] would make me tell
them how much I lack of a man." (Act 3, scene 4)
hart/heart confusion
14. *Grotesque*
Malvolio with his yellow stockings and crossed garters, smiling.
15. *Allusions*
Malvolio's description of Olivia's handwriting:
"These be her very C's, her U's, and her T's."
Malvolio's allusions to what he thought was Olivia's letter

Conclusions

The play ends in celebration and marriage as comedies often do. I have
dealt with some of the more important humorous techniques used by
Shakespeare in *Twelfth Night*. One might go on almost endlessly applying
these techniques to the play and to Shakespeare's other comedies. I've
also discussed the social and political subtext to this work—the way it
reinforces a rather conservative (in today's perspective, that is) view of
things, especially as far as social mobility of lower elements is concerned.
There is also a radical aspect to this text, for it reveals that there are fools
to be found in all classes and even Dukes and aristocratic ladies like
Olivia can make fools of themselves, especially where love's concerned.

We still find Shakespeare funny (just as we find Greek comedies
funny) because he uses techniques that are timeless. Wordplay, misunderstandings, mistakes, clowns, fools, cowards, braggarts, insults, im-
personations, eccentrics of one sort or another—all this is the stuff of
comedy and when it comes to employing these techniques, Shakespeare
has no peer.

He may have written his works hundreds of years ago, but when we
see his fantastic collection of conceited asses, blunderers, cowards,
madcaps, drunks, bawds, and zanies, we can, alas, relate these characters
to our associates and friends, to politicians and celebrities, (and perhaps
even ourselves, as well) all too easily.

11

Huckleberry Finn as a Novel of the Absurd: Making Sense of an Existential Hero

It is not terribly daring (or original) to suggest that there is some kind of a relationship that exists between a country's national character and its sense of humor. In her seminal book, *American Humor*, Constance Rourke explains this relationship as follows: (1931,9)

> Humor is one of those conceits which give form and flavor to an entire character. In the nation, as comedy moves from a passing effervescence into the broad stream of common possession, its bearings become singularly wide. There is scarcely an aspect of the American character to which humor is not related, few which in some sense it has not governed. It has moved into literature, not merely as an occasional touch, but as a force determining large patterns and intentions. It is a lawless element, full of surprises. It sustains its own appeal, yet its vigorous power invited absorption in that character of which it is a part.

Rourke obviously feels humor is a very powerful force in society and has an important socializing role. It is shaped by character and it, in turn, helps shape character. And it reveals a good deal about the beliefs, values, assumptions and dispositions of countries.

On the Importance of *Huckleberry Finn*

That explains why most literary scholars now consider *Huckleberry Finn* to be not only a great novel but a great American novel. The book has this high valuation because of Twain's brilliant mastery of the techniques of humor, because of Twain's superb use of the vernacular and because of the light it sheds on American society and culture.

Until only a few decades ago, however, *Huckleberry Finn* was characterized as a "children's book" about the adventures of a young boy on a raft—not much different from (and perhaps not even as good as) *Tom Sawyer*. We now have re-evaluated *Huckleberry Finn*, in part due to the recognition that American literature was important and in part due to the development of American Studies and myth, ritual and symbol criticism.

Now *Huckleberry Finn* has taken a position of centrality in American literature and what was once seen as a children's book has been shown to be, once we started looking carefully, a devastating attack on slavery and many other nineteenth-century American institutions. The raft and the river are now seen as symbols of the pastoral ideal, which was to be swept away by the steamboat, the railroad and industrialization. And the language of the book is now recognized to have been a major influence on American literature.

Twain's achievement is impressive in almost every aspect. The novel is a remarkable tour de force in which Twain exploits numerous comic techniques superbly. I will discuss some of these techniques, show how Twain "*pulled them off*," and discuss their significance as far as American culture and society are concerned.

On the Matter of Irony

The novel is informed by irony. Jim, a slave and the second major character in the book, tries to escape to freedom, but instead of heading north, unwittingly travels downstream, deeper and deeper into the south and the very heart of slavery. Some scholars have been very critical of this matter and of the slapstick ending which features a *deus ex machina* involving Jim's having been freed by his owner all the time. If we look at the novel from an existential point of view, as an example of the literature of the absurd, Jim's trip makes good sense. Jim moves into the eye of the storm, so to speak, where there is a kind of tranquility and where he can best expose slavery's barbarism.

The first paragraph of the book suggests its ironical tone. In a "Notice" Twain writes: (1960, no page given)

Person's attempting to find a motive in this narrative will be prosecuted; persons attempting to find a moral in it will be banished; persons attempting to find a plot in it will be shot.

BY ORDER OF THE AUTHOR

By disclaiming any serious intent and by being funny, Twain can then show the hypocrisy, meanness and hatred in American life without fear of rebuke. Huck functions as a *fool* and like all fools, and because of his youth, ignorance and innocence, he is not held accountable for his comments. The irony in the passage quoted above and the techniques of pattern and exaggeration are found throughout the book. Twain moves from threats of prosecution to banishment to shooting for those who attempt to find anything "serious" in the story.

The Attack on Formalism

Huckleberry Finn's very name is funny—it has a country flavor to it, it very ordinary and down to earth. He is well named for he is common and ordinary. And he is well endowed with common sense that constantly puts him in conflict with the various perverse and mad pre-occupations of his society: blood feuds, slavery, and other kinds of fanaticisms. He is a good pragmatist, though he is influenced, from time to time, by Tom Sawyer who has his head full of pipedreams.

In the controversial ending of the book, which ridicules romanticism and formalism, there is a dispute between Huck and Tom about how to rescue Jim. Huck wants to use picks and shovels to dig Jim out but Tom argues that they must do it the right way, with case knives: (1960, 310)

> "Confound it, its, foolish, Tom," says Huck. "It don't make no difference how foolish it is, it's the *right* way—and its the regular way. And there ain't no *other* way, that *I* ever heard of, and I've read all the books that gives any information about these things.

It might take thirty-seven years, Tom adds, but using case knives is the correct way to rescue prisoners. Tom is a formalist in every sense of the word, a person who is a victim of convention, a somewhat rigid person who cannot adapt to new situations.

Eventually Tom decides it is okay to use picks and shovels and pretend they used case knives, which satisfies Huck, who is primarily interested in getting the job done. As Huck puts it, (1960, 310)

> When I start in to steal a nigger, or a watermelon, or a Sunday-school book, I ain't no ways particular how it's done so it's done. What I want is my nigger; or what I want it my watermelon; or what I want is my Sunday-school book; and if its a pick's the handiest thing, that's the thing I'm going to dig that nigger or that watermelon or that Sunday-school book out with; and I don't give a dead rat what the authorities thinks about it, nuther.

Huck reveals himself here as a quintessential American—he adapts himself to the situation at hand and isn't swayed by what "authorities" think. He is, in fact, his own authority—a term that is most significant when it comes to American culture (where individualism, achievement and egalitarianism are core values).

As a good pragmatist he puts things to the test. For example, he tries praying for fishhooks, but when nothing happens, he decides prayer isn't worth very much. As he puts it, "No, says I to myself, there ain't nothing in it." He refuses to believe in "spiritual gifts" that are the fruits of prayer and so he "lets it go." (1960, 15)

Attacks on Religion and the Code of Chivalry

There's a considerable amount of ridiculing of religion in the book. Twain makes fun of religious revivals, superstitions and the morality of many people. For example, Huck wasn't allowed to smoke, but the Widow Douglas, who "learned" him about "Moses and the Bulrishers" took snuff. As Huck pointed out, ironically, "that was all right, because she done it herself." (1960, 3) Much of Twain's criticism escaped notice at the time because of his tricks—Huck's bad grammar and his youthfulness and naiveté—but these criticisms were there and quite obvious to people once they started looking at the book carefully.

Twain also attacks royalty and the pretentious code of Southern Chivalry, both of which elicited awe from many Americans. When the two charlatans announce, one after the other, that they are of royal blood, a Duke and Dauphin no less, Jim and Huck are "overcome." The Duke's description of his plight is ludicrous and mocks romantic conventions savagely:

> . . . The second son of the late duke seized the titles and estates—the infant real duke was ignored. I am the lineal descendant of the infant—I am the rightful Duke of Bridgewater; and here am I, forlorn, torn from my high estate, hunted of men, despised by the cold world, ragged, worn, heartbroken, and degraded to the companionship of felons on a raft. (1960, 156)

When the Duke starts getting royal treatment from Huck and Jim, the second charlatan gets jealous and announces that he, too, is of royal blood.

> Yes, my friend, it is too true—your eyes is lookin' at this very moment on the pore disappeared Dauphin, Looy the Seventeen, son of Looy the Sixteen and Marry Antonette. (1960, 159)

Huck realizes right away, of course, that the Duke and Dauphin are both frauds, but doesn't say anything in order to avoid trouble and prevent friction.

There are a number of humorous techniques operating in the above passages. We have impostors who *do not realize* that they are discovered (by Huck, at least) for what they are. There is comic rhetoric and the revelation of ignorance reflected in the poor grammar and misspellings. Whenever we have comic impostors there is always a tension established—will they be discovered or will they get away with their deception?

In the course of their adventures the Duke and the Dauphin pull off a "nonesuch," a gag that is really an elaborate practical joke but which, in its audacity, is very close to being something from what we would now call the "theater of the absurd." The Duke and Dauphin present a show for men only in which nothing happens except that the Dauphin parades around for a few minutes nude. Twain's description of this is masterful: (1960, 193-194)

> When the place couldn't hold no more, the duke he quit tending door and went around the back way and come onto the state and stood up before the curtin and made a little speech, and praised up the tragedy, and said it was the most thrillingest one that ever was; and so he went on a-bragging about the tragedy, and about Edmund Kean the Elder, which was to play the principal part in it: and at last when he'd got everybody's expectations up high enough, he rolled up the curtain, and the next minute the king come a-prancing out on all fours, naked; and he was painted all over, ring-streaked-and-striped, all sorts of colors, as splendid as a rainbow. And—but never mind the rest of his outfit; it was just wild, but it was awful funny. The people most killed themselves laughing; and when the king got done capering and capered off behind the scened, they roared and clapped and stormed and haw-hawed till he come back and done it over again, and after that they made him do it another time.

After that, the curtain was let down, concluding the "nonesuch." The audience was extremely angry (realizing it has been taken) but decided to talk up the nonesuch and continue the joke on the townsfolk, rather than admitting it had been duped.

The second night other townsfolk were there and they also were taken. On the third night, the audiences from the first two night returned, with plenty of ripe fruit, but the Duke and Dauphin didn't come on stage at all. They took off on the raft, after having made almost five hundred dollars.

This episode is a commentary on the duplicity of the townspeople who were swayed by the "bubble" of reputation. The townsfolk were used by the confidence men who anticipated what will happen, being good judges of human nature. When Jim comments to Huck that the men are "rapscallions" he sets the stage for a mangling of history by Huck, who explains that all kings are no good. As Huck explains: (1960, 197)

> You read about them once—you'll see. Look at Henry the Eight: this 'n 's a Sunday School Superintendent to *him*. And look at Charles Second and Louis-Fourteen,and Louis Fifteen, and James Second, and Edward Second, and Richard Third, and forty more; beside all them Saxon heptarchies that used to rip around so in old times and raise Cain. My, you ought to seen Old Henry the Eight when he was in bloom. He *was* a blossom. He used to marry a new wife everyday, and chop off her head next morning. And he would do it just as indifferent as if he was ordering up eggs. "Fetch up Nell Gwynn," he says. They fetch her up. Next morning, "Chop off her head."

Huck continues on with his exposition on the lives of kings and Jim comments that just living with a Duke and Dauphin is all he can stand. Huck replies to this, "Sometimes I wish we could hear of a country that's out of kings." (1960, 199) And he adds, as an aside, that it wouldn't do any good to tell jim that the Duke and Dauphin were frauds, *especially since they weren't too far removed from the real kind*. The American democrat is speaking here; nobody is better, due to accidents of birth, than anyone else and those who claim to be superior are usually, when you investigate matters, much worse than their fellow man and woman.

But if the upper classes are shown to be ugly and immoral (as they are in many of the episodes), the lower classes are also portrayed as decadent. Pop, for example, is a drunken brute. And many of the people who live in the small towns are mean and vicious. The novel has, if you think about it, an aura of pessimism and despair about it, except that Huck's humanity and resourcefulness dominate the text and shows the possibilities in American society for people of good will. We need not always submit to the pressures towards conformity, Huck shows, and we don't always have to subvert our values.

As a realist, Huck sees the meanness and selfishness of people, and often plays upon these attributes to save Jim. Huck, on the other hand, symbolizes our capacity for goodness and selflessness, and his moral development is a demonstration that our potential for goodness can be realized.

If *Huckleberry Finn* is read as an ordinary story, even if we do marvel at Twain's virtuosity with the vernacular and his comic genius, it does pose problems. The trip down the river into the heart of slavery, Huck's alienation from society, the problems of identity that are raised and the development of Huck's moral sensibility all are problematical. But they can be explained if we don't look at the book as an ordinary novel but examine it as an existential work.

As I suggested earlier, if we think of the book as an absurdist text, Jim's trip in the wrong direction makes sense. And, of course, the nonesuch is a classic bit of the theatre of the absurd, both literally and figuratively. Let me add something here about the liberties taken with logic in the book. Jim's use (or is it abuse) of logic looks like something taken right out of the pages of Ionesco's *Bald Soprano*. In the Ionesco play, some people sitting in a room hear a doorbell but when they go to the door they don't find anyone there. This happens three times, leading one of the characters to conclude that when the doorbell sounds, nobody is there.

In the chapter "Was Solomon Wise," Huck and Jim have the following conversation. Huck has just told Jim that "Polly'voo-franzy" is the way Frenchmen say"Do you speak French?" Jim thinks this is ridiculous and Huck then tries to explain why Frenchmen speak French:

> "Looky here, Jim; does a cat talk like we do?"
> "No, a cat don't."
> "Well, does a cow?"
> "No, a cow don't nuther."
> "Does a cat talk like a cow, or a cow like a cat?"
> "No, dey don't."
> "It's natural and right for 'em to talk different from each other, ain't it?"
> "Course."
> "And ain't it natural and right for a cat and a cow to talk different from *us*?"
> "Why, mos' sholy it is."
> "Well, then, why ain't it natural and right for a *Frenchman* to talk different from us? You answer me that?"

Jim's rebuttal is magnificent.

> "Is a cat a man, Huck?"
> "No."
> "Well, den, dey ain't no sense in a cat talkin like a man. Is a cow a man?—er is a cow a cat?"
> "No, she ain't either of them."
> "Well, den, she aint got no business to talk like either one er the other of'em. Is a Frenchman a man?"
> "Yes."
> "*Well*, den! Dad blame it, why doan he *talk* like a man? You answer me dat." (1960, 103)

This passage, with all its bizarre logic and misunderstandings is as much a satire on logic and the dialectic process as is the dialogue in *The Bald Soprano* showing that when the doorbell sounds, nobody is there.

I would also suggest that just as Twain's use of the vernacular in the passage quoted above can be seen as an affront to "refined" sensibilities (and a means towards a trenchant social criticism), the absurdities in *Huckleberry Finn* do not weaken it but strengthen it. I would say the same about the controversial ending of the book. Huck's alienation from his society has been commented on by numerous critics; It is asserted that in the ending we do not have an adequate solution to the problem of how a person of morality and good will is to relate to a corrupt situation in which he (or she) finds himself—other than by flight. Twain, it is said, offers no solutions to the problems he finds and no alternatives.

I don't think it is the task of imaginative literature to offer solutions to social and political problems; it is enough if a novel points out the evils that exist in a society, an act which suggests the need for reforms and changes. Huck's relation to American society and his famous statement that he is going to "light out for the territory ahead of the rest, because Aunt Sally, she's going to adopt me and sivilize me, and I can't stand it, I been there before" (1960, 374) can be explained in a number of ways.

First, there is the matter of the westering impulse and the Frontier, where one could find opportunity and, one assumes, a better moral climate (in "the Garden" or the American wilderness) than can be found in society. Huck has seen enough of society not to want much more of it. The escape to Nature, we must recall, is a dominant motif in American literature and thought. The corruptions of European society (which has influenced and debased American society) can be avoided; one can reject Europe and history, which gives the world Henry the Eight, Dukes and Dauphins, and start a new, moral, "natural" society in the wilderness.

Second, there is the mythological dimension to seeking a new territory. When Huck Finn decides to "light out" for a new territory, he is moving from profane space and profane society to a new society, what might be described as a sacred society. It is often said that *Huckleberry Finn* is an inititation story, but this initiation extends beyond teaching Huck about life and death. When Huck Finn light out, he moves into the mythic realm, and develops a stature suitable to one who has been on the river, the "brown" god.

Mircea Eliade explains the meaning of the "new territory" concept in his classic study, *The Sacred and The Profane*. He writes: (1961, 31)

> An unknown, foreign and unoccupied territory (which often means 'unoccupied by our people') still shares in the fluid and larval modality of chaos. By occupying it and, above all by settling it, man symbolically transforms it into a cosmos through a ritual repetition of the cosmogony.

Settling a territory is the same thing as consecrating it, Eliade adds, and by doing this one gets in touch with absolute reality—which is, that is, the reality of the sacred. When one inhabits a new territory and consecrates it, one moves into what is called "The Center of the World." There are, of course, an infinite number of these centers because they do not represent geometrical space but existential space.

There is a quest element to *Huckleberry Finn* but it is a quest for this Center of the World, not for some Holy Grail or anything like that. As Eliade points out: (1961, 184)

> Those who have chosen the Quest, the road that leads to the Center, must abandon any kind of family and social situation, any "nest," and devote themselves wholly to "walking" toward the supreme truth, which in highly evolved religions is synonymous with the Hidden God, the Deus absconditus.

Huck's initiation and his quest are one—he must probe the nature of the universe and to do this he must light out for the territories where he will be *enlightened*. His initiation into life has been incomplete; his rite of passage down the river, through the "straight and narrow gate" does not end when he is "born again" as Tom Sawyer. Huck Finn must be educated in the most profound sense of the term, which means educated into the sacred nature of life.

There is a great deal of death in the book, which is characteristic, Eliade tells us, of initiation rites. He writes: (1961, 191)

> In the scenarios of initiations the symbolism of birth is amost always found side by side with with that of death. In initiatory contexts, death signifies passing beyond the profane, unsanctified condition. . . . The mystery of initiation gradually reveals to the novice the true dimensions of existence; by introducing him to the sacred, it obliges him to assume the responsibility that goes with being a man.

Huckleberry Finn, then, is an inititiatory novel and, as such, leads Huck on to its logical conclusion, the discovery of a self and the growth and responsibility that stem from this awareness.

When Huck moves on, then, he is not so much escaping from his aunt and from a decadent and corrupt society as he is moving, existentially, into the Center of the World, where he will attain consciousness of higher levels of existence. As such, his actions are paradigmatic of the essential American experience, from the old Frontier to the New Frontier, from the mysteries of the Garden to the mysteries of outer space. Huck's alienation from a corrupt society is not a symptom of personality loss but of his authenticity as a person. His actions should be seen not as flight so much as an attempt to sanctify his existence. In this respect, also, he is a model for many who came after him.

12

Healing with Humor:
A Laugh a Day Keeps the Doctor Away

A number of years ago the San Francisco Symphony Orchestra faced a tricky problem. People were forgetting to turn the alarm functions on their digital watches off and from time to time a watch went off, disrupting the concerts. Someone wrote a humorous poem for the Symphony on the matter:

An Alarming Situation

T'was the night of the concert
and all through the hall,
Not a creature was stirring;
by music enthralled.
The banners were hung
from the ceiling with care.
In hopes that the best sounds would
move through the air.
But what's that we hear . . . that sound
. . . beep-beep-beep!
The noise of alarms to rouse one
from sleep.
It's worse than a blooper,
worse than a cough.
PLEASE WATCH YOUR WATCHES
AND TURN THEM ALL OFF!
(Thank you)
                                        Anonymous

This might not be great poetry, but it tells us something interesting: the symphony management thought it should use humor as a way of alerting people to this alarm problem and dealing with the matter.

Humor, we see, has instrumental qualities and is a good way of dealing with certain kinds of problems. In this situation, the problem was relatively minor but in other cases, as we shall see, humor helps us deal with more complicated and troubling matters. Humor helps us deal with difficulties, but it is also, we must remember, a source of pleasure, something we delight in.

We love to laugh, and this desire to be amused, to experience humor and the laughter that is generally associated with humor is universal and, it would seem, insatiable. No matter how much we've laughed at a comedian or during a film, we want to laugh more, and are always ready for the next gag, the next cartoon, the next funny play or television program or film. It would seem that there's a biological aspect to our hunger for humor. Without being aware of what humor is doing to us and for us, we search it out to deal with needs that we often don't even know we have.

For Humorists, Nothing is Sacred

Humor is a force that respects nobody; nothing is too revered, too holy to be ridiculed, and nothing is out of boundaries as far as humorists are concerned. Humor sheds light on our darkest secrets, and thumbs its nose at the objects of our greatest reverence. Humorists parody, ridicule, and make fun of sex, religion, love, marriage, children, society, politics—you name it, and they've been doing this throughout history. In this respect, consider the following story:

> *A tailor goes on a trip to Europe. During his trip he goes to Rome and while visiting the Vatican he sees the pope up in his balcony, blessing the multitudes below. Later on, when back in America, he's at a party and telling friends about his trip. "We saw the pope, too," says his wife. "It was really incredible." "What did you think of his holiness?" asks a friend. "A medium, size 37," replies the tailor.*

Because humor is so ubiquitous, because it plays so large a role in our daily lives, people tend to take it for granted. And, until recently, we've dismissed it as a relatively unimportant phenomenon. (For many scholars, ironically, the more people do something, the less importance is assigned to it.) But now we've begun to recognize that humor not only entertains us but is also good for us—in a number of ways.

In this chapter I will deal with the way that humor affects our health on four levels:

1. I will consider its biological aspects.

2. I will deal with its intrapsychic or intrapersonal effects and offer an explanation of how humor heals, of how it helps us, as individuals, cope with our everyday problems.

3. I will deal with humor's role in our interpersonal relationships, and will show that it plays an important role (and one which we generally don't recognize) in helping us deal with other people.

4. And finally, I will deal with the way humor helps people cope with anxieties and difficulties on the social and cultural level.

A Laugh a Day Keeps the Doctor Away

Let me start by discussing the biological value of humor and laughter. When we laugh we actually exercise our hearts and other muscles and, in addition, release endorphins, so that humor (and laughter) has physiological consequences that are of considerable value.

As William Fry explained in a lecture (1979) "Using Humor to Save Lives",

> Mirthful laughter has a scientifically demonstrable exercise impact on several body systems. Muscles are activated; heart rate is increased; respiration is amplified, with increase in oxygen exchange—all similar to the desirable effects of athletic exercise. Stress is antagonized by humor in both its mental or emotional aspect and its physical aspect. Emotional tension, contributing to stress, is lowered through the cathartic effects of humor.

Humor, then, has direct physiological and psychological benefits for individuals. The well-known work of Norman Cousins, who used humorous films and other works to recover from a serious illness has been documented in his book *Anatomy of an Illness as Perceived by the Patient* (1979). Since the publication of his book, the notion that humor has an important role to play in our physical health is now fairly well accepted. We often talk about laughter being "the best medicine." If laughter isn't the best medicine, it certainly is very good medicine.

How Humor Heals on the Intrapsychic Level

In my glossary I dealt with the basic techniques of humor. They are important because, it is the techniques used in many jokes and other examples of humor that are most significant, not the subject or content of the humor, per se. To show how humor helps people deal with psychological difficulties I will: list a few of the more important (from a therapeutic perspective) humorous techniques, say something about what each technique teaches us, and offer an example of the technique in a joke or some other form of humor.

I believe we learn indirectly by laughing at absurd and ridiculous kinds of behavior reflected in humor, behavior that is often the source of psychological problems or difficulties we all face from time to time. Thus, when we laugh at this behavior, we are, generally without being aware of it, laughing at ourselves and doing something to help ourselves. That is one of the reasons that we seek humor out so much.

TECHNIQUE: *Overliteralness, Rigidity*

FUNCTION: Making fun of rigid, inflexible behavior is an important technique. It shows the absurdity of mechanical, nonflexible or overly structured behavior and suggests the value of noncompulsive, non-obsessive behavior in others and in ourselves. The "moron" jokes are typical examples of this kind of behavior. The following poem makes the point beautifully:

The Death of John O'Day

Here lies the body
of John O'Day
Who died maintaining
the right of way.
He was right, dead right,
As he walked along.
But he's just as dead
As if he had been wrong.

Anonymous

TECHNIQUE: *Misunderstanding*

FUNCTION: Humor involving misunderstanding shows that problems of communication are enormous, that many people often misunderstand one another so we shouldn't be too harsh on ourselves or feel unusual if we have difficulties in communicating with others. A classic example would be Abbott and Costello's famous "Who's on First" routine. Here's a joke based on misunderstanding:

A young schoolteacher is on a bus and notices a man whose face seems familiar. She smiles at him, but he stares blankly at her. On the way out she turns to him and says "I'm sorry, but I thought you were the father of one of my children."

TECHNIQUE: *Absurdity*

FUNCTION: Absurd humor reflects the illogical nature of human beings and their institutions, suggests that many people have somewhat bizarre and eccentric aspects (to put it mildly) to their personalities, attacks destructive solemnity and overly harsh and overly self-critical reason. George Santayana said "the universe is an equilibrium of idiocies" and this notion helps us gain, I would argue, a good perspective on things

In Lewis Carroll's *Alice in Wonderland* we find the following passage:

"Which reminds me," the White Queen said, looking down and nervously clasping and unclasping her hands, "we had such a thunderstorm last Tuesday—I mean one of the last set of Tuesdays, you know." Alice was puzzled. "In our country," she remarked, "there's only one day at a time." The Red Queen said, "That's a poor thin way of doing things. Now here we mostly have days and nights two or three at a time, and sometimes in the Winter we take as many as five nights together—for warmth, you know." "Are five nights warmer than one night, then?" Alice ventured to ask. "Five times as warm, of course." "But they should be five times as cold, by the same rule." "Just so!" cried the Red Queen. "Five times as warm *and* five times as cold."

TECHNIQUE: *Allusions*

FUNCTION: Allusions show that large numbers of people do ridiculous things, make mistakes, and that this kind of behavior is not only widespread but natural. We need not feel, therefore, too burdened by the mistakes we make and we should not allow our consciences to torture us since "to err is human." Allusions are often found in gossip columnists and in the monologues of comedians such as Johnny Carson and Mark Russell. These allusions tease others and help us ease our own feelings of guilt.

The process is similar to what certain Hindu doctors do when they compose fairy tales to deal with problems their patients have. Bruno Bettelheim explains the matter in *The Uses of Enchantment: The Meaning and Importance of Fairy Tales:*

In a fairy tale, internal processes are externalized and become comprehensible as represented by the figures of the story and its events. This is the reason why in traditional Hindu medicine a fairy tale giving form to his particular problem was offered to a psychologically disoriented person, for his meditation. It was expected that "through contemplating the story" the disturbed person would be led to visualize both the nature of the impasse in living from which he suffered, and the possibility of its resolutions (1976, 25).

I believe that humor functions in ways analogous to the fairy tales invented by the Hindu physicians that Bettelheim mentions and that from the enormous amount of humor to which we are exposed, without being conscious of what we are doing, we select humor that will help us deal with the problems we face.

Humor's Role in Interpersonal Relationships

Not only does humor help us deal with our own difficulties, it also helps us in our relationships with others. Looking at the world and people from a humorous perspective (from a "what fools these mortals be" frame of reference) helps downgrade the "seriousness" of some things we do and say (and things others do and say) that otherwise might be looked upon as hostile or insulting. Humor thus helps dilute and cover up the hostility we might feel toward others or that others might feel toward us.

Humor also "depressurizes" us and diffuses the anger we feel when we find ourselves in relationships with difficult or, in extreme cases, poisonous people. A good laugh helps us recognize how ridiculous it is to get excited about matters that are often trivial, at least on the face of things. We recognize, of course, that many disputes over seemingly trivial things are really about matters of much more consequence (power, dominance, etc.) but even these matters often aren't worth the energy they take. Thus, a good laugh often functions as a safety valve and helps us deal with anger and anxiety.

Humor has the power to distort and confuse things, so that people who really don't like one another and should be antagonists often don't recognize this. Poor communications, in some cases, then, is functional and humor can muddy the waters and prevent hostilities from erupting.

Finally, humor often distracts people who might enter into hostile relationships by finding acceptable scapegoats. The argument here is that people redirect their aggression to these scapegoats (Poles, Jews, women, ethnic minorities) rather than focusing on one another. This distraction helps people who are hostile or feel anxiety deal with their problems other than in direct, interpersonal ways.

The Political and Social Dimensions of Humor

Not only does humor help us on the intrapsychic and interpersonal levels, it also plays a role on the social and political level. What it does, I suggest, is help us collectively deal with social and cultural phenomena that trouble us.

Let me return to a case history discussed earlier. In a study of elephant jokes made in 1969, Alan Dundes and Roger D. Abrahams, two folklorists, suggested that these jokes helped Americans deal with anxieties they felt about blacks and the Civil Rights movement in America. In their article, "Elephantasy and Elephanticide," which appeared in *The Psychoanalytic Review* (1969, 56,2) they offered a number of elephant jokes:

Why do elephants wear springs on their feet?
So they can rape flying monkeys.

What's the most fearsome sound to a flying monkey?
Boing, boing!

Why did the elephant marry the mosquito?
Because he had to.

Elephants, the authors point out, come from Africa, which is where most blacks or African Americans come from and, in these jokes, they are decidedly "super-sexual" animals. (This is one of the common stereotypes of African Americans.) The authors also list other jokes that deal with the sexuality of African Americans and suggest that we have transferred our feelings about the "threat" we felt that they posed to us, during the Civil Rights movement, onto these elephants.

One could make the same kind of argument about the other joke cycles that have become popular—jokes about Poles, light bulbs, (which were a spinoff from the Polish jokes) and so on. Thus, whenever there is a popular joke cycle, there generally is some widespread kind of social and cultural anxiety, lingering below the surface, that the joke cycle helps people deal with.

Wisdom from Folly

This notion—that we learn many valuable lessons from humor—is not new. The fools in Shakespeare's plays see things realistically but their ironic fate is that they are not taken seriously. The same thing, we might argue, happens to our present-day comedians, who are unacknowledged "instructors" for mankind and womankind. This use of humor to "instruct" is very old, it turns out. As Conrad Hyers points out in *Zen and the Comic Spirit* (1974), for hundreds of years Zen masters have made use of humor in their teaching. Is it not possible to argue, I ask, that our humorists and comedians are, without realizing it, modernized versions of Zen masters who teach us, entertain us, and, at the same time, help heal us, or perhaps it is more accurate to say help us heal ourselves.

These humorists don't recognize what they are doing. They are, in a strange way, therapists who speak, unknowingly (but not, if they are clever with words, unwittingly) to the human condition. The joke, so to speak, is on them. Humor fosters creativity, helps prevent obsessive behavior, encourages playfulness and openness, purges us of violent emotions or feelings of excessive guilt, reveals that authority is often invalid, liberates us, helps promote social cohesion, and provides great pleasure. Like any tool, of course, it can be misused, and it sometimes is; but for the most part it is an instrument of great power and utility, a gift that makes our lives not only bearable but also, thanks to its magic, enjoyable. Humor is life serving and life enhancing, which is why those who choose life also choose laughter.

13

Comedy and Creation:
On the Generative Power of Humor

There is a good deal of controversy about what humor is and isn't, but whatever it is, humor seems to be intimately connected with creativity, whatever that might be. Evidence shows that the relationship that exists between humor and creativity is a strong one and people who are creative frequently have a well developed sense of humor. As Avner Ziv writes in *Personality and Sense of Humor*,

> Many research projects have been focused on finding differences between persons who are high and low in creativity. In studies in which the humor variable has been introduced, it has clearly been shown that those high in creativity are (as a group) more open to humor than those low in creativity. Correlations between humor and creativity are positive and statistically significant. (1984, 132)

In the same light, people who are humorous are often creative.

The reason for this is that the characteristics associated with humorists are, to a great degree, the same as those associated with creative people. I am speaking of such matters as imagination, inventiveness, inspiration, originality, wildness, and spontaneity. It seems reasonable to assume that with humorists these characteristics become focused on making people laugh or creating funny material. With those who are not humorists (or, at least, professional humorists), these qualities become channeled into other directions—which lead to new ideas and discoveries.

To a great degree it is the point of view that is crucial. For the professional humorist, everything is exploited for its comic potentialities; for the creative person, everything is exploited for its creative potentialities. But the mental processes and points of view seem the same in the creation of humor and in other forms of creative behavior.

Humor as a Form of Creation

I have suggested earlier that play is intimately connected with humor. This idea was developed by Freud in *Jokes and Their Relation to the Unconscious*. In this work he writes,

> Play—let us keep to that name—appears in children while they are learning to make use of words and to put thoughts together. This play probably obeys one of the instincts which compel children to practice their capacities. . . . In doing so they come across pleasurable effects, which arise from a repetition of what is similar, a redis- covery of what is familiar, similarity of sound, etc., and which are to be explained as unsuspected economies in psychical expenditure. It is not to be wondered at that these pleasurable effects encourage children in the pursuit of play and cause them to continue it without regard for the meaning of words or the coherence of sentences. Play with words and thoughts, motivated by certain pleasurable effects of economy, would thus be the first stage of jokes. (1963, 128)

Wordplay—which we find in witticisms, nonsense humor, and other forms of humor—is intimately connected by Freud with "thought" play, which I would like to suggest is an important element of creative effort.

The play element is central. How we direct that play determines, to a great degree, whether we end up with humor or some other kind of creative effort. It is the frame of mind that I am talking about here. Humorists and creative people are usually "on" all the time, looking for ways to use whatever they can for their own devices.

Arthur Koestler also deals with humor and creativity in *Insight and Outlook*. He writes,

> To begin a book on the psychology of the higher mental functions with a detailed analysis of the comic may seem a roundabout and unorthodox approach . . . there is a . . . consideration which may help to justify the mental effort expended on an apparently so recondite subject;—namely, that in most languages the words which refer to comic invention also refer to *creative thought* as such. In the three main European languages "wit," "*esprit*," and "*Witz*" (or "geistreich") all have this double meaning. . . . Obviously "wit" in the comic sense has close affinities with "wit" in the original sense of the word, and we are led to expect that an investigation of the specific type of mental activity involved in the creation of comic stimuli will lead us to the very core of the process of creative thought itself. (1949, 15)

The notion, then, that humor is related to creativity is held by many people. But what is the relationship and what is it about humor that facilitates creativity?

One important element, I think, involves boundary breaking. Creative people have to learn to disregard the assumptions we have about things, to break conventions, to look at things from new perspectives. There's something challenging, individualistic, idiosyncratic (maybe even innocent) about the creative effort, and the same applies to humor. We value humorists for the pleasure and happiness they bring us, on the most immediate level, and for their minds and the quality of their imagination, in the final analysis. Performance is important but it is the quality of the humorist's mind that captivates us most, I would argue.

"Where do they get those crazy ideas?" we ask ourselves. "How do they think that stuff up?" The answer, I would suggest, is that humorists train themselves to see the world from a comic or comedic perspective and learn how to emphasize the creative and ludic aspects of their personalities. Also, the protection afforded them by being humorists (and therefore not being taken seriously), allows them to move beyond the boundaries of convention and at times good taste, as well. Nothing is sacred to the humorists and it is this attitude that is crucial in the final analysis. There is a kind of daring and courage we find in the great humorists and great creative people that is, quite likely, intimately connected to this privileged position they occupy in society.

Some humor can best be described as weird. (Think, for example, of *The Far Side*.) The same may be said of the ideas of some of our most creative people. This may be connected, actually, to so-called childish elements in the personalities of professional humorists and creative people. Just as children, Freud tells us, play with words and sounds without much regard for their meaning, so do comedians and creative people play with ideas. The goal is also pleasure—from seeing new relationships, from gaining new insights, from enjoying the free play of imagination and from developing inventions, new solutions to problems, and so on.

Learning to be Funny

I don't think anyone is born funny. What happens is that some people learn how to be funny, for one reason or another. People develop their capacities to be funny in order to cope with problems, to help socialize with others, to earn a living, and to deal with anxieties and hostility, among other things. But we have to learn how to be funny just as we have to learn most everything else. And we usually learn how to be funny by a process of trial and error.

I've had a good number of San Francisco comedians come to my classes over the years and have talked with them extensively about their work. Most of them say they have to work very hard to develop their material and that they are continually trying new material out to see whether it goes over or not. There is, then, at once something practical and pragmatic about creating humor and something wild and experimental.

But first comes the decision to be funny. What that means is one adopts a stance toward the world, a point of view. And that point of view is to look for the humorous side of things, to search for the comic possibilities in anything and everything. And ultimately to develop a distinctive comic identity. For stand-up comedians, this identity involves a comic persona connected to the kind of material the comedian does best. One thinks here of insult humor and Don Rickles or of victim humor and Rodney ("I don't get no respect") Dangerfield. But I'm also talking about literary humor and the importance of style. People like Perelman, Benchley, Gogol, Ionesco, Bulgakov, and West come to mind here, but there are countless others.

In the same light I think some people decide, whether consciously or not, to emphasize the intuitive, imaginative, inventive elements of their personalities—what we now believe is connected to the right side of their brains. These people opt, then, for creativity, boundary breaking, and related phenomena in contrast to those who opt for conformity, conventionality, security, and other similar values.

Once the stance has been decided upon, and often this is unconscious and perhaps the result of chance (at least to a certain degree), the rest of the process follows somewhat mechanically, strangely enough. The humorists figure out and apply the techniques of humor that work best for them and are most conducive with their personalities.

And here again the play element becomes important, because a crucial aspect of being funny involves technical matters such as revising, rewriting, editing, and reworking. In a fascinating documentary called *Woody Allen*, Allen talks about the steps he follows in creating humor. The first thing he does is to get a rough draft down. That's the hardest part, he says. But once he has the draft, he then revises the manuscript to get it right. This involves countless rewrites. It is somewhat mechanical but it also involves a highly developed and discriminating comedic sensibility to get the desired effects. It is in the editing process that the material is perfected and the idea turned into a work of art.

Editing, revising, and rewriting all have playlike aspects to them and give a kind of pleasure in their own right. They also provide a kind of anticipatory pleasure as creators envision how others will respond to their work.

The Unconscious and Comedy

The relationship that exists between jokes (and humor in general) and the unconscious is a complicated one. There seems to be a relation between aggressive tendencies and humor. In *Beyond Laughter*, Martin Grotjahn argues that humor involves masked aggression and writes,

> The wit technique overcomes inner resistance and removes inhibition by camouflaging the original aggression in a clever way, using methods of disguise similar to those used in dream symbolization. The disguise of the original aggression tendency facilitates the expression of aggression. (1966, 12–13)

What happens, according to Grotjahn, is that an aggressive impulse is first created, then suppressed, and then released in a modified way that helps the humorist evade feelings of guilt (which would be generated by the superego, were it not duped).

Humorists are people who, in a special way, have access to their unconscious and, in particular, to the id aspects of this unconscious. They are much more in touch with (or victims of?) their impulses, their aggressive tendencies, and are not as inhibited as others. This capacity to overcome restraints others feel may, I would suggest, facilitates the creation of humor and other forms of creative behavior. Many people who have the capacity to have the "wild ideas" of humorists simply do not allow themselves to do so; they are not impulsive enough. They are prisoners, in a sense, of their superegos.

In addition, there seems to be an ability to regress to childlike stages, when play and fantasy play important roles in our lives, in creative people. The wordplay and thought play and inventiveness of childhood are channeled and focused.

And it is the sense of humor, I believe, that facilitates this access to the unconscious and regression in the service of creativity. With many people, or, at least, those who have not learned to channel their creative capacities, a great deal of energy is required to repress these urges. With the creative personality, logic would suggest, the energy that most people use to keep themselves repressed (or their urges repressed, to be more specific) is free to be channeled into other areas—such as discovery, invention, and creative behavior of all kinds.

Humor may also facilitate sublimation, the rechanneling of energy from one kind of satisfaction to another. Thus, one might take one's sexual energy and direct it elsewhere, to painting, composing, writing, inventing, and so on. Sublimation is important in much contemporary thinking about creative behavior and there is reason to believe that humor helps people sublimate and achieve substitute gratifications. Humor is, itself, a source of pleasure. But humor also liberates, eases feelings of guilt, forces one to recognize the ironical and absurd nature of life, and doesn't allow people to take themselves too seriously. And these qualities make it possible to rechannel energy without too much difficulty.

Finally, there is the matter of risk taking that must be considered. Being a humorist always involves a great deal of risk, for the humorous material (the joke, the pun, the witticism) may fall flat and not elicit the response which the humorist seeks to generate. Stand-up comedians talk about "bombing" with audiences, which means striking out, not getting laughs, not going over. The alternative is "knocking 'em dead."

Stand-up comedians, in particular, must learn to live with a great deal of anxiety; they must learn to risk a great deal at every performance and not take failure as catastrophic. The same applies to all humorists, actually, but it is the performers who suffer the most direct anxiety. I would suggest that one of the characteristics of the creative individual is the capacity to tolerate high levels of anxiety and to engage in high-risk activities. Creative people learn to accept failure and not be devastated by it.

In this light, humor may help a person be more creative since humor also involves discovering ways of living with anxiety (and temporary setbacks) and risk, and may, in fact, be a good kind of basic training for the development of creative behavior.

Illusions about Humor and Creativity

Many people have rather simplistic ideas about humor. Because comedians *seem* so natural, and with the good ones, so effortless, people often think that humor is unpremeditated. This is not the case at all.

Comedians only seem to be spontaneous. In truth, a great deal of effort goes into being funny and the "ease" of humorists is really the triumph of illusion over reality.

A number of years ago I happened to be passing a comedy nightclub in San Francisco and found the proprietor conducting a class in stand-up comedy. There were a number of comedians standing around watching a videotape monitor. Their "bits" had been taped and now were being evaluated. There are, it turns out, a great many things to be considered by performers: their timing, their props, their facial expressions, their body language, their voice quality, their use of language, their ideas, their comic personas, and so on. There was a great deal of animated discussion about each of these matters.

Other forms of humor are equally difficult and that simple piece of nonsense we laugh at from Benchley or Woody Allen may be, in fact, the tenth rewrite of the piece. Stand-up comedians, as a rule, do very little improvising and humor writers don't usually submit first drafts of manuscripts that have come right off the top of their heads.

Just as many people undervalue and underestimate the amount of effort involved in creating humor, they overvalue the amount of genius involved in other forms of creative behavior. Artistic, literary, and scientific creation is seen by many (perhaps because it is often portrayed that way by the media) as being, in some sense, a gift of the gods.

The notion that the creative person is, in some ways special, has been with us for a long time. In *Modernity and Its Discontents*, Cesar Graña writes about nineteenth-century attitudes toward genius. If we substitute "the creative person" for genius in the quotation that follows, we can see that attitudes have not changed a great deal. Graña writes,

> Genius was unleashed as an all-powerful, radical and unequaled event, a gift of nature which must be allowed to take its course no matter how disruptive to common perceptions. It was now not only the right of intelligence to be respected but also the duty of genius to tear up norms, to shatter the confines of rules and to permit a whole new world of reality, uniquely perceived, conceived, and expressed, to emerge out of its oceanic depths. (1976, 52)

Creativity is seen as magical, remarkable, a gift bestowed on just a few individuals who are then to be treated specially and to whom the norms of conduct do not apply.

While there may be an element of truth to this romantic view of creative behavior in some cases, more often than not creative achievement is the result of hard work and an enormous expenditure of effort. There is reason to think that creative people see work as play and thus can expend a great deal of effort and concentration to achieve their objectives. The saying that genius is 90 percent perspiration and 10 percent inspiration is very much to the point here.

Perhaps the best way to put things is to suggest that humor isn't as easy as it seems and other forms of creative behavior aren't as magical as we might imagine. Artists and other kinds of creative people aren't terribly interested in attacking this romantic notion of creation, for it serves them well. But it also leads people to devalue their own creative potentialities.

A question suggests itself here. Are only certain people who are "beloved of the gods" creative or can everyone be creative? The answer, of course, hinges on our definition of creative. Though not everyone is an artist or a poet or a professional humorist, I believe everyone has creative capacities. Every time we dream, and we generally dream every evening, we are being creative. And every time we make a jest, say something funny, or make a pun, we're being creative. I don't think creativity applies only to certain domains (painting, sculpture, literature, science, music, etc.) as much as it does to attitudes and approaches to things. One can be a creative accountant (and the truly creative ones are in great demand) or industrialist or an uncreative painter. In this respect I recall a wonderful cartoon from *The New Yorker*. A couple is sitting in an art gallery that reminds one of a diner. The owner has pulled open a window and is shouting an order to an artist, in a back room, in a manner analogous to the way in which waitresses shout orders to cooks:

One lyrical landscape—heavy on the Wyeth, light on the Expressionism.

Comedy, Chance, and Creativity

Jack Benny developed his famous "cheapskate" persona virtually by accident. What we have is a wonderful instance of the role of chance in a person's career and the way an idea can be played with and developed creatively. After years of listening to the program everyone knew that Benny was cheap. What they didn't know was how this cheapness would manifest itself, what remarkable twists and turns it would take, how it could be applied, adapted, modified, stretched, and manipulated for some forty years or so.

There seems to be reason to believe that an element of chance and accident exists in scientific discovery and other forms of creative activity. Newton sees an apple fall and goes on to discover gravity or a laboratory worker makes a mistake and a new medicine is found. Friedrich August Kekulé is supposed to have had a dream (of a snake with its tail in its mouth) which revealed to him the shape of benzene. What is important here is that these accidents or chance events be used and exploited for their potentialities and not just dismissed out of hand.

Humorists, like all creative people, live in a world of chance, where things might be different, and where random happenings and accidents suggest possibilities to be explored and developed. Every joke, after all, has a punch line that involves surprise. Jokes, and other forms of comedy, condition us to expect things to be different at times from what we anticipate, and this predisposes us to be innovative and creative.

This point was made by Frederic Flach, a psychiatrist, in *Creative Psychiatry*, a pamphlet he wrote for psychiatrists that was published by Geigy pharmaceutical. He discusses a patient of his and writes,

> The appearance of humor was a break in his armor and a clue to the emergence of some creativity. . . . Humor, then, is itself a form of creative activity, and the emotional discharge which accompanies it, in the form of laughter, is intimately associated with the surprise element in discovery. In this patient it became possible, through the judicious use of humor, to stimulate what little innovative abilities he possessed and thereby consider himself differently in the context of his life. (1975, 13–14)

Flach also suggests that psychiatrists exercise more creativity in their treatment of patients and use whatever methods seem most appropriate, including trying new modalities and being more innovative.

On Satisfactions and Creative Behavior

One of the most important gratifications creative people get is a sense of pleasure from achievement, discovery, and success. But the process is also important. This point is made by William F. Fry, Jr. and Melanie Allen in their essay "Humor as a Creative Experience: The Development of a Hollywood Humorist." They discuss the notion that creativity is seen by many as, in essence, a process and write,

> For those who argue that the process IS the creativity, the patterns or combinations are seen merely as ephemeral way-stations in the process or by-products of it. They characterize creativity as the pursuit of an objective that must always elude complete realization. The reach is more important than the grasp. (1975, 246–247)

There is pleasure in the process of creativity and there is pleasure in the fruits of the creative process. This would explain why stand-up comedians are willing to risk bombing with audiences. When the comedians don't bomb they experience a powerful feeling of exhilaration and perhaps power, as well, since comedians make people laugh. I would imagine that creative people, in general, feel the same kind of thing; a sense of triumph in having done something special, in having achieved some goal or made some kind of a mark.

There is also a strong element of being a benefactor, of having done something for others. Creative people often derive a sense of pleasure from having contributed something to others and this is a very powerful motivation. Humorists are continually thinking about their audiences and how these audiences can be reached. I would suspect that the same sense of doing something useful and beneficial for others is found in most creative people. They may pursue their work in a single-minded manner and even seem to be selfish or egocentric, but in the long run there is something altruistic about their actions.

This is not to deny that financial considerations must be taken into account. First-rate professional humorists, of all kinds, are exceedingly well paid. There is a voracious hunger in the general public for humor—perhaps because people instinctively recognize that humor plays an important role in their lives and helps them deal with stress and anxiety. Inventors often make fortunes from their work, and so do creative accountants and industrialists.

But I don't think it is only the financial rewards that generate creative efforts. To a great degree it is the pleasure derived from the process of creation and the personal gratifications that creative people get that are of primary importance. There is also the element of status. Creative people are generally awarded high status—perhaps because the creative process is such a mystery. Whatever the case, there is considerable psychological payoff for creative people and this may, in fact, play an important role in helping people develop the creative potentialities they have. As the title of this chapter suggests, humor is a form of creative activity and it is a form that, I believe, facilitates and generates other kinds of creative behavior. If this is true, then it seems logical that we can learn how to use humor to develop our creative potentialities.

Bibliography

Abrams, M.H. *A Glossary of Literary Terms*. New York: Holt, Rinehart & Winston, 1961.

Adams, J. *Ethnic Humor*. New York: Manor Books, 1975.

Allen, S. *Funny Man*. New York: Simon & Shuster, 1956.

Apte, M.L. *Humor and Laughter: An Anthropological Approach*. Ithaca, NY: Cornell University Press, 1985.

Alter, Robert. *Rogue's Progress*. Cambridge, MA: Harvard University Press, 1964.

Ashbee, C.R. *Caricature*. London: Chapman & Hall, Ltd., 1928.

Ausubel, Nathan. *A Treasury of Jewish Humor*. New York: Doubleday, 1951.

Ausubel, Nathan. *A Treasury of Jewish Folklore*. New York: Crown Publishers, 1978.

Bakhtin, Mikhail. *Rabelais and His World*. Bloomington: Indiana University Press, 1984.

Becker, Stephen. *Comic Art in America*. New York: Simon & Schuster, 1959.

Bennett, D.J. "The Psychological Meaning of Anti-Negro Jokes." *Fact* (1964).

Berger, Arthur Asa. *Li'l Abner: A Study in American Satire*. New York: Twayne Publishers, 1970.

Berger, Arthur Asa. "Was Krazy's Creator a Black Cat?" *San Francisco Examiner (This World Magazine)*, 22 August 1971.

Berger, Arthur Asa. *The Comic-Stripped American*. New York: Walker & Co., 1973.

Berger, Arthur Asa. "The Secret Agent." *Journal of Communication* 24 (1974).

Berger, Arthur Asa. *The TV-Guided American*. New York: Walker & Co., 1975.

Berger, Arthur Asa. "Huck Finn as an Existential Hero." *Mark Twain Journal* (Summer 1976).

Berger, Arthur Asa. "Anatomy of The Joke." *Journal of Communication* (1976).

Berger, Arthur Asa., ed. "Humor, The Psyche and Society" *American Behvioral Scientist* 30, no. 3 (January/February 1987).

Berger, Arthur Asa. "Comics and Popular Culture." *The World & I* 5, no. 7 (1990).

Bergler, Edmund. *Laughter and the Sense of Humor*. New York: Intercontinental Medical Book Co., 1956.

Bettelheim, Bruno. *The Uses of Enchantment: The Meaning and Importance of Fairy Tales*. New York: Knopf, 1976.

Blair, Walter. *Native American Humor*. San Francisco: Chandler Publishing Co., 1960.

Boatright, Moady. *Folk Laughter on the American Frontier*. New York: Collier Books, 1961.

Boskin, J. *Humor and Social Change in Twentieth Century America*. Boston: The Public Library of the City of Boston, 1979.

Botkin, B.A. *A Treasury of American Folklore*. New York: Crown Publishers, 1944.

Brody, M. "The Wonderful World of Disney—Its Psychological Appeal." Unpublished manuscript, 1975.

Cameron, William Bruce. *Informal Sociology*. New York: Random House, 1963.

Cantril, Hadley, and Gordon W. Allport. *The Psychology of Radio*. New York: Peter Smith, 1941.

Capp, Al. *The Life and Times of the Shmoo*. New York: Simon & Schuster, 1948.

Chapman, Tony, and Hugh Foot., eds. *Humor and Laughter: Theory, Research and Applications*. London: John Wiley & Sons, 1976.

Charney, Maurice. *Comedy High & Low*. New York: Oxford University Press, 1978.

Cousins, Norman. *Anatomy of an Illness*. New York: W.W. Norton & Co., 1979.

Davies, Christie. "An Explanation of Jewish Jokes about Jewish Women." *Humor* 3-4, (1990).

Davies, Christie. *Ethnic Humor Around the World*. Bloomington: Indiana University Press, 1990.

Douglas, Mary. *Implicit Meanings: Essays in Anthropology*. London: Routledge & Kegan Paul, 1975.

Duncan, H.D. *Language & Literature in Society*. Chicago: University of Chicago Press, 1953.

Dundes, Alan, and Roger Abrahams. "On Elephantasy and Elephanticide." *The Psychoanalytic Review* 56, no. 2 (1969).

Dundes, Alan. *Cracking Jokes: Studies of Sick Humor Cycles and Stereotypes.* Berkeley, CA: Ten Speed Press, 1987.

Eliade, Mircea. *The Sacred and The Profane.* New York: Harper, 1961.

Esar, Evan. *The Humor of Humor.* New York: Bramhill House, 1952.

Esar, Evan. *The Comic Encyclopedia.* Garden City, NY: Doubleday, 1978.

Feinberg, Leonard. *The Satirist: His Temperament, Motivation and Influence.* Ames: Iowa State University Press, 1963.

Felheim, Marvin., Ed. *Comedy: Plays, Theory and Criticism.* New York: Harcourt, Brace & World, Inc., 1962.

Flach, Frederic. *Creative Psychiatry: The Creative Process in Psychiatry.* Ardsley, N.Y.: Geigy Pharmaceutical, 1975.

Freud, Sigmund. *Jokes and Their Relation to the Unconscious.* New York: W.W. Norton & Co., 1963.

Freud, Sigmund. "Character and Anal Eroticism." In *Sigmund Freud: Character and Culture,* edited by Philip Rieff. New York: Collier Books, 1963.

Fry, William. *Sweet Madness: A Study of Humor.* Palo Alto, CA: Pacific Books, 1963.

Fry, William, and Melanie Allen. *Make 'Em Laugh: Life Studies of Comedy Writers.* Palo Alto, CA: Science & Behavior Books, 1975.

Fry, William. "Using Humor to Save Lives." Address to the American Orthopsychiatry Association, 1979, Washington, D.C.

Fry, William, and Waleed A. Salameh., eds. *Handbook of Humor and Psychotherapy.* Sarasota, FL: Professional Resource Exchange, 1986.

Frye, Northrop. *Anatomy of Criticism.* Princeton, NJ: Princeton University Press, 1957.

Graña, Cesar. *Modernity and Its Discontents.* New York: Harper, 1976.

Grotjahn, Martin. *Beyond Laughter: Humor and the Subconscious.* New York: McGraw Hill, 1966.

Gruner, Charles. *Understanding Laughter: The Workings of Wit and Humor.* Chicago: Nelson-Hall, 1978.

Harrison, Randall. *The Cartoon: Communication to the Quick.* Beverly Hills, CA: SAGE Publications, 1981.

Hebdige, D. *Subculture: The Meaning of Style.* London: Methuen, 1979.

Helitzer, Melvin. *Comedy Writing Secrets.* Cincinnati: Writer's Digest Books, 1987.

Highet, Gilbert. *The Anatomy of Satire*. Princeton, NJ: Princeton University Press, 1962.

Hoffman, D.G. *Form and Fable in American Fiction*. New York: Oxford University Press, 1961.

Hoffman, Werner. *Caricature from Leonardo to Picasso*. London: John Calder, 1957.

Howe, Irving, and Eliezer Greenberg., eds. *A Treasury of Yiddish Stories*. New York: Schocken, 1974.

Hyers, Conrad. *Zen and the Comic Spirit*. Philadelphia: Westminster, 1974.

Kayser, Wolfgang. *The Grotesque: In Art and Literature*. Bloomington: Indiana University Press, 1963.

Klapp, Orrin E. *Heroes, Villains and Fools: The Changing American Character*. Englewood Cliffs, NJ: Prentice-Hall, 1962.

Klein, Alan. *The Healing Power of Humor*. Los Angeles: Jeremy P. Tarcher, 1989.

Koestler, Arthur. *Insight and Outlook*. New York: Macmillan, 1949.

Kris, Ernst. *Psychoanalytic Explorations in Art*. New York: International University Press, 1952.

Legman, Gershon. *Rationale of the Dirty Joke*. New York: Grove Press, 1968.

Levin, Harry. *Playboys and Killjoys: An Essay on the Theory & Practices of Comedy*. New York: Oxford University Press, 1987.

Levine, Jacob., ed. *Motivation in Humor*. New York: Atherton Press, 1969.

Lodge, David. *Modern Criticism and Theory: A Reader*. New York: Longman, 1988.

Lynn, Kenneth. *Mark Twain and Southwestern Humor*. Boston: Atlantic Little-Brown, 1959.

McGhee, Paul E., *Humor: Origins and Development*. San Francisco, CA: W.H.Freeman & Co., 1979.

McGhee, Paul E. and Jeffrey H. Goldstein. *The Handbook of Humor Research*. New York: Springer-Verlag, 1983.

Mendel, Werner., ed. *A Celebration of Laughter*. Los Angeles: Mara Books, 1970.

Mindess, Harvey. *Laughter & Liberation*. Los Angeles: Nash Publishing, 1971.

Monroe, D.H. *Argument of Laughter*. Melbourne: Melbourne University Press, 1951.

Morreall, J. *Taking Laughter Seriously*. Albany: State University of New York Press, 1983.

Peter, Laurence J., and Bill Dana. *The Laughter Prescription*. New York: Ballantine, 1982.

Piddington, Ralph. *The Psychology of Laughter*. New York: Gamut Press, 1963.

Plessner, Helmuth. *Laughter and Crying*. Evanston, IL: Northwestern University Press, 1970.

Powell, Chris, and George E.C. Paton., eds. *Humour in Society: Resistance and Control*. New York: St. Martin's Press, 1988.

Propp, Vladimir. *Morphology of the Folktale*. Austin: University of Texas Press, 1979.

Raskin, V. *Semantic Mechanisms of Humor*. Dordecht: D. Reidel, 1985.

Rosenheim, E.W. *Swift and the Satirist's Art*. Chicago: University of Chicago Press, 1963.

Rosten, Leo. *The Joys of Yiddish*. Harmondsworth, England: Penguin, 1971.

Rourke, Constance. *American Humor: A Study of National Character*. New York: Doubleday Anchor Books, 1931.

Saussure, Ferdinand de. *Course in General Linguistics*. New York: McGraw-Hill, 1966.

Schickel, Richard *The Disney Version*. New York: Avon Books, 1968.

Sypher, Wylie., ed. *Comedy*. New York: Doubleday Anchor Books, 1956.

Twain, Mark. *Huckleberry Finn*. New York: Washington Square Press, 1960.

Vernon, Enid., ed. *Humor in America: An Anthology*. New York: Harcourt Brace Jovanovich, 1976.

West, Nathanael. *Miss Lonelyhearts*. New York: Avon, 1964.

West, Nathanael. *A Cool Million and The Dream Life of Balso Snell*. New York: Avon, 1965.

Wiesel, Elie. *Souls on Fire*. New York: Vintage Books, 1973.

Wilson, Christopher P. *Jokes: Form, Content, Use and Function*. London: Academic Press, 1979.

Wolf, Michelle A. and Al Kielwasser. eds. *Gay People, Sex and the Media*. Binghamton, New York: The Haworth Press, 1991.

Wolfenstein, Martha. *Children's Humor: A Psychological Analysis*. Bloomington: Indiana University Press, 1964.

Worcester, David. *The Art of Satire*. Cambridge: Harvard University Press, 1940.

Yates, Norris. *The American Humorist: Conscience of the Twentieth Century*. Ames: Iowa State University Press, 1964.

Ziv, Avner. *Personality and Sense of Humor*. New York: Springer, 1984.

Ziv, Avner. ed. "Introduction." *Humor* 4-2, 1991.

Names Index

Subject Index

Jokes and Humorous Texts Index

① A Primer on
Jungian Psychology

② Like A Donkey
Between two bundles of
Hay.

③ Madness - Religion
Experience & the
Wisdom to know
The Difference